THE

McGRAW-HILL
36-Hour Course

ORGANIZATIONAL
DEVELOPMENT

D1024638

ORGANIZATIONAL
DEVELOPMENT

Stephen R. Balzac

New York   Chicago   San Francisco   Lisbon   London   Madrid   Mexico City
Milan   New Delhi   San Juan   Seoul   Singapore   Sydney   Toronto

Copyright © 2011 by The McGraw-Hill Companies, Inc. All rights reserved. Printed in the United States of America. Except as permitted under the United States Copyright Act of 1976, no part of this publication may be reproduced or distributed in any form or by any means, or stored in a database or retrieval system, without the prior written permission of the publisher.

1 2 3 4 5 6 7 8 9 10 11 12 13 14 15 16 17 18 19 20   QFR/QFR   1 9 8 7 6 5 4 3 2 1 0

ISBN   978-0-07-174382-2
MHID   0-07-174382-0

This publication is designed to provide accurate and authoritative information in regard to the subject matter covered. It is sold with the understanding that neither the author nor the publisher is engaged in rendering legal, accounting, securities trading, or other professional services. If legal advice or other expert assistance is required, the services of a competent professional person should be sought.
        —*From a Declaration of Principles Jointly Adopted by a Committee of the American Bar Association and a Committee of Publishers and Associations*

Library of Congress Cataloging-in-Publication Data

Balzac, Stephen.
        McGraw-Hill 36-hour course organizational development / Stephen Balzac.
        p.   cm.
        ISBN 978-0-07-174382-2 (alk. paper)
        1. Corporate culture.   2. Organizational behavior.   3. Organizational effectiveness.   4. Management.   I. Title.   II. Title: Organizational development.

        HD58.7.B355   2011
        658—dc22   2010019135

Trademarks: McGraw-Hill, the McGraw-Hill Publishing logo, 36-Hour Course, and related trade dress are trademarks or registered trademarks of The McGraw-Hill Companies and/or its affiliates in the United States and other countries and may not be used without written permission. All other trademarks are the property of their respective owners. The McGraw-Hill Companies is not associated with any product or vendor mentioned in this book.

Portions of Chapter 1 appeared in slightly different form in the January/February 2010 issue of *Analog Science Fiction and Fact* under the title "Take Off Your Hat: You're in the Presence of Culture." Portions of Chapter 3 appeared in slightly different form in the *Worcester Business Journal* under the title "How to Avoid Becoming Dilbert's Pointy-Haired Boss." Portions of Chapter 4 appeared in slightly different form in the *Journal of Corporate Recruiting Leadership* under the titles "The Godot Effect," "7 Things You Should Communicate," and "Communicating with Retention in Mind." Reprinted with permission from ERE.net. Portions of Chapter 4 also appeared in the *Worcester Business Journal* under the title "Becoming a Talent Magnet" and in the *IndUS Business Journal* under the title "How You Hire Just as Important as Who You Hire." Portions of Chapter 5 appeared in slightly different form in the *Worcester Business Journal* under the title "The Motivation Trap" and in *CareerSmart Advisor* under the title "How to Effectively Motivate Your Team." Portions of Chapter 6 appeared in slightly different form in the *Journal of Corporate Recruiting Leadership* under the title "Stalking the Elusive Leader: The Role of Emotions in Recruiting." Reprinted with permission from ERE.net. Portions of Chapter 8 appeared in slightly different form in *Lab Manager Magazine* under the title "I Told You: 360-Degree Feedback Done Right." Portions of Chapter 9 appeared in slightly different form in *Mass High Tech* under the title "Five-Step Process to Making Change Work." Portions of Chapter 11 were originally presented at the Infotec technology conference under the title "Organizational Culture and Innovation: A Two-Edged Sword." Portions of Chapter 12 were originally presented at the 2005 SENG national conference under the titles "Cartesian Splits and Chinese Splits" and "Relaxation to Rev Up and Rev Down" and in *CareerSmart Advisor* under the title "How to Make Meetings More Productive Endeavors."

McGraw-Hill books are available at special quantity discounts to use as premiums and sales promotions or for use in corporate training programs. To contact a representative, please e-mail us at bulksales@mcgraw-hill.com.

This book is printed on acid-free paper.

CONTENTS

INTRODUCTION

What is management by intention? It sounds like a bit of an oxymoron. After all, don't we do everything by intention? Well, yes and no.

One of the lessons of competitive sports, like the highly competitive world of business, is that what we do does not always produce the results we expect, no matter how much our action feels "right" or intentional. In the course of some twenty years of working in high tech, I have consistently found similar patterns of intentionality and lack of intentionality in the office. As a consultant, I've found CEOs who manage by magic spell: they found something that worked once and attempt to repeat that success in every new situation. When it doesn't work, they blame their employees. What is happening, of course, is that they are in a situation that reminds them of a previous situation, and without thinking about it, they respond to the new situation as they did in the past. They think they are acting intentionally, but they are actually on automatic pilot. They are reacting, not acting.

The goal of this book is to provide you with the knowledge of the patterns of organizational behavior that will enable you to act intentionally, not merely react. We will look at organizational development from the broad, encompassing frame of organizational culture and explore the specific skills you need to develop in order to shape and direct your organization.

In the end, intentional management is understanding the organization as a living, dynamic system. It is understanding how our decisions in one area can produce unanticipated effects in an apparently unconnected area. Intentional management is learning to be aware of the undercurrents and interactions in an organization so that we can choose the effects we want. When we are acting, as opposed to reacting, we are solving the problems and facing the challenges that are in front of us, not the ones the organization faced six years, six months, or six days ago. Intentional management is the art of overcoming the real challenges, not the illusions.

Good luck!

ACKNOWLEDGMENTS

To my wife, Aimee, and children, Adira and Ilan. Thank you for your patience and support while I was working on this book and, in Ilan's case, not climbing on me too often while I was writing!

THE ───
McGRAW-HILL
36-Hour Course

ORGANIZATIONAL
DEVELOPMENT

CREATING THE CULTURE

Most courses don't cover organizational culture, or just briefly describe it as "the way we do things around here." Unfortunately, this cavalier attitude only creates difficult, expensive problems. Your organization's culture is not something to take lightly. All attempts at organizational development will both be influenced by the culture of the organization and will influence that culture. Everything, from how you recruit and hire employees to how you handle rewards and punishments to how you build teams, conduct meetings, manage conflict, deal with competition, and so on, will both reflect and affect your culture.

WHAT IS CULTURE?

So if culture is not "the way we do things around here," what is it?

Culture is the frame within which we operate and the lens through which we view the organization. If we view an organization as a system of interacting and interrelated parts, culture defines, creates, and supports that system. But this definition is only the tip of the iceberg.

The Taboo of the Bananas

There is an oft-told, albeit probably apocryphal, study involving four gorillas. The gorillas are placed in a cage with a ramp at the top of which is a bunch of bananas. As soon as one of the gorillas starts to go after the bananas, high-pressure water hoses are turned on, knocking the gorilla off the ramp and soaking all of them. This happens until no gorilla will go near those bananas. At this point, the hoses are removed, and one of the gorillas is replaced by a new gorilla. When the new gorilla tries to get the bananas, the other gorillas all jump on him and drag him back. This continues until that gorilla has learned to not go after the bananas. Eventually, the cage contains four gorillas, none of whom has ever been hosed but none of whom will go near the bananas. Whether or not this story is true, it does accurately capture some fundamental concepts of culture.

At only the most superficial level, culture is "the way we do things around here." As MIT professor Ed Schein, expert on organizational culture and father of organizational psychology, points out, it is extremely danger-ous to assume that's all there is to culture. Focusing only on the "what we do" yields a superficial understanding that all too frequently leads to costly, painful problems for the organization later. Cultural change efforts that focus only on the "what" are doomed to failure before they've even begun. The more significant questions are, why is that the way we do things? In what way does it benefit us to do things in a particular fashion? In the case of the first set of gorillas, the Taboo of the Bananas meant not getting hosed. How-ever, that's no longer the case for successive generations. For them, passing on the Taboo of the Bananas means that they don't get beaten up by their fellow gorillas. The hoses are gone, and all that remains is the tradition that the bananas are forbidden.

Ultimately, what culture is doing is providing us with a map of how the world works. As such, culture serves to tell us how we fit into the world and teaches us how to behave, be successful, be happy, and so forth. Culture is what Schein describes as an "anxiety-reducing agent." As such, culture is extremely resistant to change. Changing a culture means changing our fundamental view of how the world works. IBM ran into serious financial difficulties in the late 1980s and early 1990s in large part because it was unwilling to change the ways in which it was approaching the market, even though the market was rapidly changing around it. Think about your own organization: when has the organization resisted change because that meant breaking with tradition?

The Residue of Success

The question still remains, what is culture? Ed Schein defines culture as "the residue of success," the accumulated wisdom of what does and does not work in dealing with the world. Although this seems like a simple, straightforward definition, it requires some explanation. Success is not always what it appears to be. Our gorillas, for example, have achieved success in learning how not to get hosed. They, at least, have created a cultural tradition that has its roots in an actual causal relationship. That is not always the case.

A significant force in cultural development is *post hoc ergo propter hoc*. That is, people assume that the success of a particular action is due entirely to how that action was performed or what they did immediately before the action, and not to external forces or even actions performed weeks or months ago. Thus, a rain dance is believed to bring rain or the wearing of a particular outfit will bring success in battle.

What we see is that the *perception* of cause and effect is enough to cause a behavior to become a cultural value. Assuming that the behavior and the result occur together often enough, the behavior will come to be taken for granted. Members of the culture will no longer question the behavior because, within that culture, it is now a basic tenet of how the world works. Other cultural values will arise to support and enable the behavior. In the end, a simple behavior leads to an interlocking network of beliefs, assumptions, and values. Attempting to change any piece is extremely difficult because every other piece attempts to pull it back into place. Cultures, whether at the familial, organizational, or societal levels, do not change easily.

HOW IS CULTURE CREATED?

Modern cultures do not spring forth out of nothing. Cultures build on existing cultures. A new business may create its own unique corporate culture, but that business is not starting with a blank slate; rather, it is inheriting its initial culture from the dominant culture in which it is located and the cultural values brought by the founders and early employees. It is thus possible for a culture to inherit from multiple parent cultures.

Forming Subcultures

Cultures also differentiate, or form subcultures, based on specific situational needs. Ed Schein observes that all businesses form three distinct subcultures: executives, engineers, and operators. The executive subculture is concerned with making the organization run, the engineers with solving the problems faced by the organization, and the operators with actually implementing the solutions and dealing with the outside world. Executives create rules and mechanisms to make the organization function smoothly—we call it bureaucracy. Engineers seek to develop elegant solutions that cannot be screwed up by people. (As evidence, despite all the complaints and problems with batteries in Apple's iPods, the iPhone still does not have a user-replaceable battery. To design a product with one would violate a cultural belief about making the device elegant and hard to damage. As a further example along those lines, Apple now sells a new laptop that does not have a user-replaceable battery.)

On a larger scale, subcultures form in response to organizational needs, geographical constraints, and anything else that requires adapting to various environmental conditions. A large corporation, such as IBM, has subcultures broken out by country and task. Countercultures also form within the larger culture. A *counterculture* in this context is a subculture that deliberately rejects certain aspects of the parent culture while still remaining committed to the parent culture's goals. For example, during IBM's blue suit and tie heyday, the research division was determinedly informal. Unlike the rest of IBM, jeans and T-shirts were common, and ties were rare.

How Leaders Shape Culture

Within an organization, leaders have tremendous power to shape the culture through a variety of means. At the most basic level, the example a leader sets will form the basis for much of the culture. The culture of the once mighty Digital Equipment Corporation (DEC) reflected the beliefs and attitudes of its founder, Ken Olsen. DEC was once the darling of the computer industry, an incredibly successful company during the 1960s, '70s, and into the '80s. It was, in many ways, the Microsoft of its day, the company that many believed would destroy IBM. Today it no longer exists. Olsen, an MIT-educated engineer, believed that all ideas should be tested through argument and debate; if the idea couldn't be proved wrong, the developers had the right to go ahead with the idea and let the market decide. This approach served DEC very well in its early days. However, because Olsen never really believed in the PC, the culture at DEC was to not take the PC seriously. As a result, and because no one group could convince the other groups they were wrong, DEC ended up producing three different, incompatible versions of the PC. The net result was that the market decided not to support any of DEC's PCs. What a leader pays attention to and how a leader responds to a crisis, deals with disagreement, treats those around him, and behaves in general will all feed into the culture of the organization.

If, as I've often seen, a leader treats every unexpected problem or unanticipated roadblock as a major crisis, so will the employees. If a leader takes the view that every problem could have been avoided and therefore when something goes wrong, heads must roll, the resulting culture will usually be one of blame and finger-pointing. If a leader views mistakes as a natural part of learning, exploring, and experimenting, the resulting culture is likely going to be one that supports innovation.

Beyond actions, leaders shape the culture through the stories that they tell and the stories that are told about them. The stories a leader tells help to inform employees about what the leader considers important. At one start-up I worked for many years ago, the CEO used to talk disparagingly about his interactions with the customers. Every customer was an idiot, an incompetent, or both. It wasn't long before this attitude permeated the company. The effects could be seen in every area, from the engineers writing the software, to tech support, to marketing, and so on. Sloppy design decisions were made because, after all, the customers were "too stupid" to know the difference.

Even when the founder, or other influential leader, is no longer around, his or her legacy lives on, reinforcing the values of the culture. When I worked for IBM many years ago, there were countless stories about Tom Watson: how when an IBM employee was badly injured and his family killed in a car accident, Watson was there at the hospital when the man woke up, promising to cover the medical bills and do whatever he could; how, when a train derailment injured a large number of IBMers on their way to the World's Fair, Watson drove out in the middle of the night to organize the rescue effort; and other such anecdotes. These stories underscored the cultural meme that IBM took care of its employees no matter what. Stories like these, whether told at one of the largest companies in the world or at a small nonprofit, serve to reinforce and transmit the organization's culture.

HOW IS CULTURE TRANSMITTED?

Culture is transmitted in a variety of ways. For our gorillas, the transmission is through being beaten up by other gorillas if you happen to go after those bananas. More generally, though, cultures are transmitted through formal and informal means. Formal methods include education, religion, and family values. Informal methods include stories, songs, artifacts, and social signals.

Education is a fundamental tool of cultural transmission, be it societal or organizational culture. What American students are taught in school shapes their understanding of American culture; what employees are taught on the job shapes their understanding of their corporate culture. Sometimes, these may be in contradiction to aspects of the larger culture.

The artifacts of our culture include stories, songs, institutions, symbols, and buildings. Artifacts can also include how we use time, where we park, how we address others, where people live, and any other choice that might be made within the domain of the culture. The artifacts are constant reminders of how culture works and what it stands for. The meanings of those artifacts, however, may change or may be viewed differently by different groups within the culture. One of the most difficult tasks for a newcomer to a culture is to determine what meanings the artifacts have; it doesn't matter whether the culture in question is a foreign country or a new corporation. For example, having a parking spot near the doors might be a sign of high status in one company, meaningless in another, and low status in a third. Offices on higher floors of a building sometimes indicate higher status.

WHAT ARE THE ADVANTAGES AND DISADVANTAGES OF CULTURE?

To digress briefly, the concept of automaticity is extremely familiar to athletes and teachers. A skill is said to be *automatized* when one can perform that skill with little or no conscious effort. Think of a basketball player dribbling a ball, or a student reciting a poem from memory. In each case, the actions are so ingrained that they are executed automatically when the appropriate stimulus is presented. Relatively complex series of actions can be practiced and automatized, a process sometimes referred to as "chunking." The advantage is that the chunk can be performed without calling upon cognitive resources. The disadvantage is that an automatized chunk is very hard to change; it's even difficult to interrupt yourself once the chunk is triggered. If you are interrupted, it's often extremely disorienting and virtually impossible to pick up where you left off. Instead, you usually have to start again at the beginning. Cultures operate in an analogous fashion: sequences of behavior come to be taken for granted, and once started, cannot easily be stopped. The advantage of this is that resources are not constantly expended reanalyzing the same situation. The disadvantage is that the situation may be more nuanced than the chunked behavior can handle.

Cultures also provide members with common ground in a set of shared and agreed-upon values and beliefs. The stronger and more prevalent these values are, the easier it is for members of the culture to work together and form strong bonds among one another. Culture thus acts as a unifying force among people who are steeped in the culture but can be a repulsive force for those who are not. Thus, new members to the organization, that is, new members of the culture, need to be educated as to the cultural values and how those values are manifest.

What makes understanding culture particularly difficult is that two cultures can develop completely different ways of manifesting the same stated values. For instance, both the PC and the Mac claim to be easy to use. They both are, but in very different ways, and for very different audiences. PC hardware and software can be easily customized by the user, provided that user is reasonably knowledgeable about the technology. The PC user can do almost anything but can also screw up the system quite thoroughly. The Mac, on the other hand, provides a very slick, clean interface that may limit what you can do but also prevents major disasters. Similar cultural values, very different results.

Ultimately, a culture can be thought of as an encapsulation of concepts, values, and behaviors. Members of a culture will default to the culturally determined heuristics if they haven't developed a more specific version or override of their own. The reasons behind the values and behaviors are hidden within the encapsulation and become "it's just how we do things."

WHAT MAKES A SUCCESSFUL CULTURE?

A culture is successful if it is in harmony with its environment and unsuccessful if it is unable to function in its environment. The environment is the world in which the culture operates. Here's the catch: environments change faster than cultures. When the environment changes, the mechanisms of the culture may no longer be valid. As we've already discussed, a culture is an encapsulation of information and procedures for dealing with the world. The advent of the PC changed the business environment for IBM, and the company found it difficult indeed to adjust. The bursting of the tech bubble in 2000 turned Sun Microsystems from one of the world's top companies to one that could not function in the brave new post-bubble world. Today, with the accelerating shift from desktop computers to mobile devices and the Internet, Microsoft is still, in many ways, playing catch-up. Just because those procedures are no longer working doesn't mean that they immediately fall out of favor. First, the procedures are chunked, so they are carried out at an almost reflexive level. Second, the prospect of change can, and often does, engender more fear and anxiety than the actual failure of the outmoded procedures. Acknowledging that these fundamental cultural lessons are wrong is tantamount to admitting that the world does not work the way we thought it did. Some cultures can adjust; others cannot. A third, and potentially more serious, issue is that the world, and human behavior, is not digital: it is not either 1 or 0. In other words, rarely does a behavior go from working 100 percent of the time to not working 100 percent of the time.

Rapid environmental change is not instantaneous. Rather, the change occurs over a period of time. A behavior that worked most of the time in the old environment starts failing more and more frequently. Initially, this is hard to distinguish from the normal, occasional failures. The initial reaction is to "try harder" while doing the same thing. So long as the behavior still works sometimes, periodically these increased efforts, these "sales drives" or what have you, will appear to be making a difference. This is a phenomenon known as *intermittent reinforcement*, and, in this context, it creates an illusion of success. A set of behaviors that are reinforced intermittently can become even more ingrained than they were before the intermittent reinforcement began!

Thus, as the environment moves away from the culture, the culture's reflexive efforts to apply the lessons of success can actually lock the culture into increasingly nonfunctional behaviors! In general, the best way to change a culture as the environment changes is not to introduce something new but to strengthen an existing aspect of the culture.

In 1992, IBM imploded. The company posted a loss for the first time in its history, closed down numerous divisions, and even instituted layoffs. IBM's survival was in serious question. However, IBM's culture contained a very strong ethic of "analyze the problem, determine the solution, and execute the solution even if it's unpleasant." IBM realized that it needed a fresh perspective, so it brought in Lou Gerstner, the first non-IBMer to become CEO. As Ed Schein points out, Gerstner came from a very similar marketing background to IBM's founder, Tom Watson, Sr. Gerstner didn't so much change IBM's culture as revitalize an aspect of it that had become dormant. Over the years, IBM's engineering culture had become dominant, and the marketing culture had faded into the background. In restoring the latter, Gerstner also restored the company's fortunes.

WHERE IS CULTURE?

Culture is in the minds of the people who comprise the culture. When a culture is threatened by something in its environment, be that a new idea or another culture, it becomes more *itself.* In other words, those cultural elements that appear to be most appropriate to reducing the anxiety are triggered to deal with the threat. More diverse cultures are likely to attempt multiple simultaneous solutions, while more monolithic cultures are more likely to view all problems as nails for which they are the hammers.

For example, let's look at a company called "Shrinks-R-Us," or SRU for short. (The company and example are real, but the name and various descriptive details have been changed to preserve anonymity.) SRU provides mental health services and is paid primarily through insurance. Over the years, SRU developed a system of paperwork that is the envy of bureaucrats everywhere. Why? No one seems to know, and it no longer matters. What matters is that today paperwork is seen as the answer to every problem. If employees make too many mistakes or attempt to streamline the process, the company adds another layer of paperwork. One therapist commented that the paperwork is so complex they have to use checklists—meta-paperwork—to make sure that they've done it all. There is even a quality-assurance committee that reviews the internal paperwork with a fine-toothed comb, sends back anything with an error, and puts out weekly reports that people are expected to read. The bulk of therapists' time is controlled by the need to do the paperwork. Quality is no longer about the success of therapy, but the accuracy of the paperwork. Fundamentally, the culture has developed the organizational equivalent of obsessive-compulsive disorder (OCD).

Now, compare SRU to "ShrinkWrap," another company in the same mental health industry and in the same broad geographic area. (Again, the company's name and various identifying details have been changed where necessary to preserve anonymity.) Both SRU and ShrinkWrap host a number of psychology interns at their sites. Both are required to provide supervision and training for the interns, which includes reviewing their notes and treatment plans and monitoring their work with patients.

ShrinkWrap requires that interns keep notes, as does SRU. However, that is about the limit of the paperwork at ShrinkWrap. At SRU, in the words of one intern, "I couldn't sneeze without running it by my supervisor." At Shrink-Wrap, on the other hand, interns sometimes wonder if anyone even knows what they are doing. However, as one intern observed, "Any time something came up, my supervisor was clearly familiar with the case." At SRU, no one is trusted to do anything right; everything must be documented, checked, and rechecked. Mistakes are not tolerated and result in an immediate decrease in autonomy through the imposition of more paperwork. At ShrinkWrap, the assumption appears to be that if you bring in competent people and educate them about what is expected, you can trust them to get it right. The inevitable mistakes will be treated as part of the learning process, and people will be quietly educated as to the correct course of action in the future.

As these examples illustrate, similar companies in similar businesses and similar geographic areas can produce extremely different cultures, but both cultures respond to stress by becoming more themselves. SRU, being more monolithic, has one response to every problem. ShrinkWrap, with its more diverse culture, tends to attempt multiple solutions simultaneously.

HOW CAN CULTURE BE CHANGED?

SRU and ShrinkWrap have developed very different ways of responding to their very similar environments. In both of these organizations, it is highly likely that the original beliefs of the founders shaped the culture into what it is today. However, when the founders move on, it is equally likely that nothing will change. Neither organization will easily tolerate a new CEO who seeks to change the existing culture too radically or too quickly.

The Cultural Immune Response

One of the problems DEC had in its later years, as did Atari, and Apple under John Sculley, was a CEO who didn't share the culture's fundamental culture. In general, the leader of a cultural entity, be that entity company or country, has tremendous power to influence the entity. However, the degree to which the leader meshes with the existing culture will determine his success. When there is a mismatch, the culture will reject the interloper in much the same way as the immune system will respond to a virus. The ideas of the leader are actively or passively opposed, and the members of the culture may leave, become discouraged, or experience other signs of stress and depression. The leader may be forced out, as happened to John Sculley, or the organization may be destroyed, as happened to DEC. There is a great deal of truth to the old belief that the health of the king is the health of the land, or at least of the organization.

Remember that culture is a road map of how the world works. The longer that culture has been in place, the more successful the organization has been, and the more people like the way things are working and are happy with the current situation, the stronger the culture will be. The stronger the culture, the more the road map is trusted. The more the road map is trusted, the harder it is to change.

When a new leader comes in who clashes with the culture, problems will immediately arise. It doesn't matter whether we're talking about a group leader or a CEO, although, in general, the smaller the group, the weaker the culture—simply because it is not distributed over as many people. What the new leader is effectively doing is saying, "Everything you know, everything you believe in, is wrong. Trust me. Follow me. I have the truth."

Now, I suspect that many of you reading that last paragraph are rolling your eyes and thinking, "Yeah, right. It can't be that big a deal!"

Let's consider the situation. For the members of the culture, this road map—this view of the world—is their common bond. It's the thing that holds the organization together. By providing structure and predictability, culture reduces anxiety and promotes a feeling of security. Remember also that culture quickly becomes largely unconscious. Behaviors are chunked, no longer thought about on a conscious level.

Then someone comes along and says, "No, no, that's all wrong." Imagine being in that position. How would you feel? How did you feel the last time your company announced major changes or restructuring?

When a new leader's approach contradicts the fundamental, underlying values of the culture, employees are caught in a state of cognitive dissonance. Very briefly, *cognitive dissonance* is a state in which people are forced to hold two or more contradictory ideas in their heads at one time. When at least some of the ideas that they are holding are not even at a conscious level, it makes the situation worse. People will seek to move away from a situation that induces cognitive dissonance. The problem is, they may not move to where you want them to go.

In this case, the new CEO is telling them to do things that they "know" in their hearts are wrong. Moreover, most CEOs will make the situation worse by engaging in logical arguments. This is a situation that is less about logic than emotion, a topic we'll cover in more depth in Chapter 7. When logic fails, as it usually will in a cultural mismatch, the CEO will often resort to threats and punishment. The employees feel increasingly trapped and resentful. Some will reluctantly comply, despite feeling guilty that they are betraying their inner beliefs and exposing themselves to the anxiety of their cultural road map not being correct. Others will try to quietly or openly undermine the CEO. Others might try keeping their heads down and hoping that the situation gets better. Some will go along and may well be seen as traitors by the rest. Some will leave. In short, the organization becomes ill.

Fortunately, there are ways to change a culture successfully!

Strategies for Successful Change

Although it is possible for the CEO or senior management to ram through changes in the culture, this will often have unanticipated consequences. Because cultural values are tightly linked, the more central the value being altered or removed, the more pressure there is to restore the preexisting cultural norm. Remember, cultures are self-reinforcing. Cultural values and beliefs support one another, and when an attempt is made to alter a cultural belief, the existing network of ideas pulls back.

The management team, however, does have the power to simply change a policy. If that policy reflects a cultural value in the company, then the change may be far-reaching and unpredictable. For example, in the mid-1990s, IBM abandoned Tom Watson's long-held policy of full employment for life: you took care of the company and the company took care of you. It was a mutually beneficial, symbiotic relationship. IBM was a rock that employees knew would always be there for them. Then it all changed. In response to changing economic conditions, IBM decided that it could no longer afford to maintain full employment. The end of full employment was the psychological equivalent of an earthquake.

In October 2009, the *Wall Street Journal* reported that IBM executive Robert Moffat, "a senior vice president and a close confidant of IBM Chief Executive Samuel Palmisano," was arrested for insider trading. While it's impossible to fully identify all the ramifications and permutations in such a complex system, when Robert Moffat was arrested, IBM discussion groups on the Net brought up the point over and over that when full employment was removed, so was the source of a great deal of loyalty to the company. The two values had become intimately tied together. While no one condoned Moffat's behavior, there was also a strong sense of "what did you expect?"

Since my approach to changing the culture is strongly influenced by Ed Schein, I'll be drawing heavily on material from Ed Schein's work, in particular *The Corporate Culture Survival Guide*.

Let's start by recognizing that cultures are constantly changing and adapting. The process, however, is generally extremely slow and usually undirected. New lessons are learned over time and incorporated into different aspects of the culture. At the same time, old lessons may fall into disuse. They are not so much forgotten as become dormant, waiting for an appropriate trigger to activate them. It can take a very long time for a behavior to be completely lost to institutional memory; it's the reason for the behavior that is forgotten quickly. Remember our gorillas: the Taboo of the Bananas persists for generations after the original reason for the "taboo" is lost.

As members of the organization work their way up through the hierarchy to positions of power and leadership, they bring with them their own particular spin on organizational culture based on their own experiences. Generally this won't be too far from the mainstream. If they appear too "out of touch" with the culture, they will not be accepted or promoted.

Promote and Recruit Hybrids

This process of gradual change can become more intentional through a conscious effort to shape the culture on the part of the existing leadership. Recall our earlier discussion on subcultures. People who spend their careers in a particular subculture will partake of both the main organizational culture and the specific subculture. By promoting people from a subculture that represents the direction the leader wants to take the organization in, the organization will, in time, move in that direction. Schein refers to such people as "hybrids."

Sometimes people will leave an organization only to be eventually lured back. These are, again, people who have "grown up" in the company but have also absorbed and become part of external organizational cultures. These *external hybrids* fit within the culture and also bring in new ideas and ways of approaching problems. Their background in the culture makes them acceptable to the people still there and also provides credibility for their new ideas. They are often recruited back when the original company realizes that it needs a fresh perspective and simultaneously the security of having an insider. It is, therefore, a very effective strategy to draw these external hybrids back.

Tell a New Story

A leader can also change the direction of a culture by gradually changing the stories. Stories always change and become embellished over time, and new stories are constantly being created. By taking an active role in this process, the leader or leaders can slowly shift the culture in a new direction.

Practice Management Jujitsu in the Face of Inertia

Sometimes, though, the culture needs to respond rapidly to a very real external threat that can destroy the organization. In this case, the leader needs to make radical changes very quickly. The danger lies in moving too quickly. Reacting without taking time to think or plan is a very bad idea unless you've developed a trained, practiced reaction to just the situation that you're now facing. Even after you've stopped to think about what you're doing and carefully considered and determined the correct course of action, you still have a limit to the speed of your reaction: the organization itself. Consider what happened in organizational change initiatives that you've experienced or observed. What events played out?

In physics, inertia is the property of an object in motion to remain in motion and an object at rest to remain at rest. Cultures have psychological inertia. Just as it is difficult to shift the course of a massive object, it is also difficult to shift the course of a large organization. Unfortunately, even a fairly small organization possesses a great deal of psychological inertia. Unlike physics, the way to shift psychological inertia is not through the application of pure force. When dealing with people, the more force you use, the more suspicious they become. Fighting through resistance wastes both time and energy when neither is precisely abundant.

In the practice of the Japanese martial art of jujitsu, an attacker is dealt with by blending with his motion and then gently redirecting him into the nearest wall. One does not oppose, because opposition only prolongs the conflict. Rather, one joins the attacker where he or she is. By the same token, you do not try to force your employees to change. Unless your organization is tiny, you will spend far more time and energy fighting the same battles over and over again, possibly for years, than you will ever save. Instead, you need to join your employees where they are. While we'll go into the processes and how-tos of these steps in more detail in subsequent chapters, there are a few key points to think about now:

• **The first step is to perform what Schein refers to as "unfreezing" the situation.** In other words, you must set the stage for what is to follow. Remember that people will cling to the existing culture because it makes them feel safe. Therefore, you need to do two things: first, highlight the dangers the organization faces. Lay out the situation. Be intense, but not panicky. Your goal is not to scare people, and if you come across as panicked, they will panic as well. Your goal is enable people to recognize the risks of the status quo. Your next step is to provide the solution: describe the desired results of the proposed changes, and then talk about how you'll get there. While you may not get everyone on board immediately, repeating the message frequently will enable you to start building critical mass.

• **Once you gauge that you've built a receptive audience, you can start making changes.** This step is very much like the slow approach in that you'll be promoting people into positions of power, changing stories and creating new ones, redefining existing symbols or eliminating them entirely, teaching people new skills and new ways of working, and so forth. The biggest difference is the speed: it'll be happening over the course of weeks or months, not years. In the event that you must eliminate some cherished company artifact or symbol, be that a slogan, a way of doing business, traditional images, company policies, etc., it is best to symbolically mark the end of that artifact. Think of it as the moral equivalent of a wake. You are celebrating the success that the artifact brought to the company and the place it holds in people's hearts, but also saying good-bye to it as well. Finally, replace it with something else.

Part of moving quickly is making sure you don't have to circle back too often to pick up the stragglers or those who got lost along the way. That means make it easy for people to learn the new skills. Provide examples, coaching, and practice, and make it possible for them to experiment and make mistakes without fear of punishment. The more you move people as a cohort, the more they will reinforce each other as the training takes hold.

The key is to make the transition as easy as possible for your employees. In the long run, the easier it is for them, the easier it will be for you and the more effective it will be for the company. Focus on positive examples whenever possible. Constantly show people where they are going and, whenever possible, recruit those who are successful to help bring others along. Should there be those who cannot adjust, who simply cannot or will not adapt to the new world order, that's OK. If they leave, either voluntarily or because you are forced to fire them, you give them a generous severance and help them find a new job somewhere else. You are investing in goodwill and your next generation of potential hybrids. Just because they couldn't adapt today doesn't mean that they won't learn to adapt somewhere else and become a valuable ally or employee again in the future.

  • **Finally, once the changes are complete, you must refreeze the situation.** Highlight the successes and make sure people know that you've arrived. Celebrate! Again, the goal is to make it easy for your employees to feel good about the new culture.

Remember, Culture Is a Habit

It's well known that there's nothing harder to do than to break a habit. Cultural behaviors are habitual behaviors, and cultural change is breaking old habits.

In sports, athletes deal with bad habits by creating good habits. They don't try to get rid of the old habit. Instead, they practice something new until it becomes stronger than the old habit. In cultural terms, that means finding an existing aspect of the culture that you can build upon and strengthen until it overwhelms the parts that are no longer adaptive. The more you can ground your changes in existing culture, the easier it will be to gain acceptance of them. You've transformed something new and frightening into something old and familiar. You still have to make it easy for people to practice the new ways of doing things, and you still need to make it easy for people to experiment and make mistakes, but you've created a sense of security from the start.

PUTTING CULTURE IN PERSPECTIVE

Culture is the biggest, most powerful, and least understood piece of organizational development. It is often ignored or minimized even as it influences every decision the organization makes. As you read through the rest of this book, consider how the various pieces fit into the culture of your organization. Whenever you find yourself thinking, "That'll never work!" ask yourself, "Why not? What would stop it?" You may have just tripped over a cultural iceberg waiting to sink your company.

Review Quiz

1. Which of the following are influenced by organizational culture?
   a. Problem solving
   b. Hiring
   c. How meetings are conducted
   d. How people address one another
   e. All of the above
2. What is culture?
   a. The way we do things around here
   b. A necessary ingredient in making yogurt
   c. The collection of lessons learned about how to be successful
   d. Habitual behaviors
   e. None of the above

3. **Culture resists change because**
   a. It's hard to break a habit
   b. Employees are an ornery bunch
   c. Culture change makes people anxious
   d. No one likes to be told what to do
   e. All of the above
4. **The advantages of culture are that it**
   a. Automatizes behaviors
   b. Provides a common frame of reference for employees
   c. Reduces anxiety
   d. a & b
   e. a, b, & c
5. **Why do failing behaviors become even more ingrained?**
   a. No one wants to admit to being wrong.
   b. Because behaviors fail gradually, they are reinforced intermittently.
   c. People like to double down.
   d. The employees are out to get the company.
   e. Cultures are the residue of failure.

2

THE SCIENCE AND ART OF GOAL-SETTING TO DEFINE THE BUSINESS

One of my favorite questions when I'm working with a company is, "What are your goals?"

The number of blank looks I get is absolutely amazing. Some people tell me that the goal of the company is to make money. That sounds good. Unfortunately, it's a bit vague. In fact, it's not even a goal. There are a lot of ways to make money, many of which have little to do with the company's culture or mission. I realize this may sound facetious, but it's actually quite significant. Vague objectives cause vague focus. The vast majority of top athletes do not focus on money or even winning; rather, they focus on perfecting their skills. They don't try to do *their* best. They know exactly what *the* best looks like, and they strive to exceed that.

WHY SET GOALS?

Like chess, the rules of goal-setting are relatively easy, but the strategies are limitless. Goal-setting is as much art as it is science. Indeed, for most of the twentieth century, formal goal-setting amounted to little more than "goals are good." Unfortunately, the concept that goals are good does not imply that you'll be setting good goals. It wasn't until 1968 that Edwin Locke asked the question "Does goal-setting affect performance?" It was more than two decades later that Locke published the paper that led to modern goal-setting theory.

The fact is, properly constructed goals are very powerful tools. Goals increase focus and concentration because you know what you're trying to do. Goals increase persistence, especially if you are getting good feedback on your progress. Goals lead to increased energy: when you know what you're trying to do, you're not wasting time and energy trying to figure it out. You are less vulnerable to distraction because you understand where you are going and what you are trying to do.

People who are pursuing well-defined goals automatically use knowledge and skills they've already acquired to accomplish those goals. They are also much more likely to seek out new information and develop new skills as necessary to accomplish their goals. The fencer who wants to increase endurance will more naturally seek out someone who can teach her the skills she needs to most effectively do that. The programmer who has a clear idea of the goals of the product is more likely to learn new engineering skills in anticipation of their need, not at the last minute.

The more you care about your goals, the more enjoyable it is to accomplish them and the more it builds your sense of competence and your sense of your own ability to influence your surroundings. This is known as *self-efficacy*. The best predictor of goal accomplishment is increased self-efficacy.

With all these benefits, you'd think that there would be a lot of happy, productive workers out there. Unfortunately, that doesn't seem to be the case. Why not?

WHAT IS A GOAL?

Most goals set in businesses are not goals at all. Most of the rest may technically qualify as goals but are so poorly structured as to be almost worse than useless. I hear all the time from people at various companies, including some very senior employees, that they don't really know what's expected of them, but that's OK because their performance reviews either never actually happen or are totally unrelated to reality.

Far too often, what passes for a goal is an instruction to "do your best." Unfortunately, as we'll see, this doesn't work. In fact, it is a recipe for erratic performance, argument, and burnout.

At the most basic level for a goal to be effective, it needs to provide people with a clear picture of what they are trying to accomplish and give them a means to obtain feedback as they work toward the goal. Think of a goal as the destination and the feedback as the landmarks and road signs along the way. How many of us would go on a drive without a map or GPS, with no knowledge of what to look for to tell us we were going in the right direction, and possibly even no way of knowing when we'd arrived? Put another way, if you don't know where you're going, you can spend a lot of time not getting there.

Yet that's what businesses are effectively asking employees to do all the time.

Goals vs. Intentions

Unless you live under a rock, each year you hear about, or quite possibly make, New Year's resolutions. Everyone makes them: get in shape, lose weight, make more money, stop procrastinating, and so on. They last a couple of months, and then they're gone. The problem is that New Year's resolutions are intentions, not goals. Some other examples of intentions include shipping the product on time, designing a successful product, doing better at work, and doing your best on all projects.

The problem with intentions is that they're too vague, too lacking in specificity, and too open-ended. There is no way to know if you're making progress or even if you've accomplished your intention. How will you know if you're "doing your best on all projects"? What does that mean?

As we'll discuss in more depth later, the perception of progress is essential to maintaining motivation. When people feel they are not making progress for long periods, they become discouraged. There's a reason why so many martial arts use a system of colored belts to measure progress: students can easily see where they are in the progression from beginner to black belt, they know how far they've come and how much further there is yet to go, and they know when they get there. Those martial arts that subscribe to the approach that you are a white belt until you get your black belt (in other words, those that provide no visible means of measuring progress along the way) generally have lower enrollment overall and far fewer students sticking it out all the way to black belt than those that do provide visible means of measuring progress.

So, how are goals different from intentions?

Fundamentally, goals are concrete, are personally important, provide feedback on your progress, are time-bound or time-delimited in some way, and are possible, and the outcome is at least in some measure under your control.

Thus, there is no point in setting a goal of winning the lottery. Beyond the simple act of buying a ticket, you have no control over the outcome.

The fact is that far too many people set goals that appear to be under their control but really are not. For example, consider the athlete who sets the goal of winning an upcoming tournament: the goal is specific and measurable, and it has a time of completion associated with it. Is it achievable and realistic? Depending on the athlete's level of skill, very possibly. However, the athlete has no control over the difficulty of the competition. He may simply be outplayed by a more skilled opponent.

Furthermore, although the goal is measurable, in that the athlete will know whether or not he accomplishes it, the measurement is not particularly useful. At no time will he know how close he is to accomplishing the goal, where he needs to focus his energies, or what else needs to be accomplished. The athlete is far better served by setting the goal of exercising certain key skills in the competition, skills that have a high probability of leading to a victory. Not only will he gain the self-confidence boost of accomplishing his goal, he may just win the tournament.

On the business side of the equation, I worked for a certain company many years ago that decided to motivate the engineers by making them responsible for how the product did in the marketplace. Seemed like a good idea, right? After all, wouldn't that give the engineers incentive to work hard to build the very best product they could? As logical as that seemed, there was one small flaw: it didn't work.

The engineers had no control over the sales of the product. That was the job of the sales team. The sales team, however, had many products to sell and overall quotas to meet. They didn't have any product-specific quotas; rather, they simply had to bring in a certain amount of business each quarter. Therefore, they sold the products that they understood the best and were most comfortable selling. No matter how good a job the engineers did, if they couldn't get the sales team to pay attention, it didn't make any difference. Add to this a cultural assumption that sales was responsible for how it allocated its resources so long as it made its quotas, and the engineers were in trouble. Their goals were largely outside their control, and the part of the process that they were able to influence gave them no useful feedback that might have helped them get their products sold. Many simply gave up in disgust and left the company.

Now, sometimes, even the most well-constructed goal will still have components that are outside your control, such as winning a competition or making a million dollars on the stock market the nontraditional way (the traditional way is actually quite easy: start with two million). In such a case, it becomes even more important to focus on the behaviors and outcomes that you can control. Just as an athlete would set goals around building endurance, practicing key skills, and training different scenarios, an engineer might set goals around learning new skills, spending a certain amount of time fixing bugs, defining good design parameters, and so forth. Our nontraditional investor might set goals around learning about the stock market, such as understanding how the market works, learning terminology, and studying the methods used by successful investors.

As you can see, there are a number of different types of goals that are involved here.

Outcome, Process, and Learning Goals

Goals can be broken down into three types: outcome, process, and learning. Each type of goal can be broken down further into subgoals of any of the three types, until the goals are small enough to accomplish. This process is known as goal decomposition, and it will be covered in more depth later in the chapter.

- **Outcome goals, or objectives.** These goals represent the point of the enterprise. This may mean shipping a product by a certain date, winning a major contract, designing a presentation, or making a fundamental alteration to the organization's culture, to name a few. Nontrivial outcome goals are, in many ways, the most difficult goals because you will not always have complete control over all the factors. While the concept of "nontrivial" is somewhat idiosyncratic, for all intents and purposes any goal that can be accomplished with no significant expenditure of time, effort, or resources can be considered trivial. We care about the nontrivial goals—the goals that often require significant effort, have sizeable payoffs, and are not always completely controllable. For example, shipping a product by April 1 could be derailed by a late-season snowstorm or a vendor failing to supply critical components on time. Winning a contract depends partially on what you do but also on the actions of other competitors, the mood of the person making the decision, and how the company is doing financially. Outcome goals are best "decomposed" into process goals, learning goals, and smaller outcome goals. Outcome goals that are not decomposed can lead to hyperfocus and missed opportunities.

- **Process goals.** These are the "how" goals. Process goals focus on desired behaviors that will help bring an outcome goal to life. Our businessman trying to win a major contract might set process goals around practicing his presentation until he's able to do it smoothly. An athlete might set process goals around practicing certain skills or engaging in specific types of training exercises. Process goals can also be decomposed into outcome, process, and learning goals. For example, the process of selling widgets can be decomposed into the process of making phone calls, the process of executing a sales pitch, the process of closing the deal, and other process subgoals.

- **Learning goals.** These are goals to acquire relevant knowledge or skills. In the course of attempting to accomplish outcome and process goals, you might find that you are missing knowledge or lacking skills you need for success. That lack would suggest the development of relevant learning goals. Learning goals can also be broken down into process, outcome, and further learning goals.

A key concept in effective goal-setting is recognizing that goals can be mixed, matched, and combined in an almost limitless variety of ways. Fortunately, there are usually a variety of paths to success.

STRATEGIES FOR GOAL-SETTING

As I've mentioned previously, goal-setting is both an art and a science. There is no magic formula. There are, however, strategies that you can use that will make the process easier. As you become comfortable with, and start seeing success from, the strategies I've suggested, experiment and figure out what works best for you.

Goal Decomposition

One of the primary reasons that goals fail is that they are simply too big. Think about any large task: shipping a product, obtaining a black belt in jujitsu, losing twenty pounds by June, running the Boston Marathon, or writing a book. Each of these projects is immense. Trying to tackle it all at once is a recipe for disaster. As the old kids' joke goes, "How do you eat an elephant? One bite at a time."

Goal decomposition is the process of breaking your goals down into manageable subgoals. As we've seen, each major goal can decompose into outcome, process, or learning goals. The less control you have over the final outcome, the more important it is to identify what you can control and develop appropriate subgoals. Remember that you can always control processes and learning opportunities. Process and learning goals also give you the most feedback on your progress and the most information for course correction or goal revision. Remember also that outcome goals will often not give you feedback until the event itself, while process and learning goals give you feedback along the way.

Another key part of effective goal decomposition is time: as you break down your goals, you'll see that they may start to form a natural progression. Goals will feed into other goals. What you're seeing is the appearance of short-term and long-term goals.

Short-term, or proximal, goals tell you what you need to do today.

Long-term, or distal, goals tell you what you need to do tomorrow.

Short-term goals are the bites you are taking from that elephant. Each short-term goal moves you forward step-by-step toward your long-term goals. As you lay out your goals, you can start assigning completion targets, or deadlines, to them. You will also start to see how some goals naturally trigger others.

Time is not a rigid target or a scarce resource to be used as efficiently as possible. It is a tool for providing you with feedback on your progress. If you're constantly missing your targets, you know that you're being too aggressive with your deadlines. If you're beating your targets by a large margin, you're not being aggressive enough. You always want to run slightly ahead of schedule, a concept we'll discuss in more depth in Chapter 12.

It helps immensely to check off your goals as you accomplish them. That simple act increases your sense of progress and makes it easier to periodically review how far you've come.

Implementation Intentions

I've spent a great deal of time telling you that intentions are not particularly useful. There is one exception: when you form intentions to work on your goals. These very specific types of intentions are known as "implementation intentions."

Accomplishing goals often requires flexibility in order to deal with the numerous problems that can arise along the way. However, the price of flexibility is the inability to quickly recognize and act upon an opportunity. Goal attainment can be dramatically improved through the use of implementation intentions to decide in advance how to respond to different situations. Athletes do this all the time when they practice dealing with different possible scenarios. A simple implementation intention would be to say, "As soon as I sit down in my chair after lunch, I will start working on the report."

Goal intentions are simply a statement of an end point. Implementation intentions specify when, where, and how the goal is to be attained. This, in turn, enables the activation of goal-directed behavior based on environmental cues instead of conscious volition. In other words, implementation intentions help you to get started and keep moving toward a goal in the face of distractions.

Furthermore, implementation intentions can be designed to specifically ignore distractions. An intention to ignore a distraction is more effective in maintaining goal-directed behavior than an intention to increase effort when the distraction occurs.

Finally, implementation intentions lead to an automatization of actions, such that actions become immediate and efficient. Because conscious intent is no longer necessary to decide what to do next, more cognitive resources are made available for goal-related or other tasks. In other words, you are setting up your environment to tell you what to do next. Completion of one event activates the next event.

For example, I coached an insurance salesman who couldn't make phone calls. As you might imagine, that is a bit of a disadvantage in the insurance game. We worked together to design a set of interlocking goals that would trigger the appropriate behaviors. Because phone calls were the biggest problem, we tackled that first. When I asked him when he felt most optimistic, most able to tackle any challenge, he told me that it was right after he did his morning run. We then designed his goals as follows:

Goal: morning run.
Goal: after morning run, make ten phone calls.
Goal: after ten phone calls, take shower.
Goal: after shower, make ten phone calls.
And so on, throughout the day.

Seems ridiculously simple, doesn't it? In fact, he all but laughed at me when I first proposed it. I convinced him to give it a try for a couple of weeks. I still remember the day he walked into my office and said, "I didn't really believe this stuff, but I promised to give it a try. It's working. I'm making all the calls I need and more. I still can't believe it!"

This stuff doesn't need to be complicated.

While on the topic of intentions, I want to take a moment now to discuss the concept of "do your best." I hear parents tell children to do their best. I hear teachers tell students to do their best. I hear coaches tell athletes to do their best. And I hear managers tell employees to do their best work.

All too often, the subsequent conversation goes something like this:

"You call that your best work?"
"Yes."
"Well, it's not!"

Alternately, here is another common result of "do your best":

"Are you done yet?"
"I'm still working on it."
"Well, you're out of time."
"But it's not done yet. I can make it better!"

The problem is, each person has a different mental image of what "best" looks like. "Best" is a highly idiosyncratic state, and without external referents, there's no way to determine what "best" really is. A perfectionist or, at the risk of being redundant, an engineer, will never feel that he is doing his best work. He'll be tinkering and tweaking and never quite finishing, making deadlines something that happen to other people. The other problem with "do your best" is that the solution that is developed thereby may be theoretically optimal, but impractical.

When you find yourself telling your employees to do their best, take that as feedback that better goal definition is in order.

HOW DO YOU MAKE GOALS MATTER TO YOU?

The effectiveness and power of goals is in direct proportion to how much the goal personally matters to you. The more the goal matters to you, the greater the degree of satisfaction and enjoyment that results from accomplishing that goal.

One of the best ways of making goals matter is to make sure that you align them with cultural values of your organization. Because members of the culture have already implicitly bought into the values of the culture, goals that support those values are already implicitly personally important.

Goals can also become relevant through tying them to your own values and beliefs and helping your employees to tie them to their values and beliefs. The greater the level of connection, the more personally relevant the goals will be.

Another way of building relevance is to help your employees see how accomplishing the goal will make a difference. The change doesn't have to be very big, nor does it have to involve many people. Sometimes, it just involves you. You can also make goals relevant through your own excitement and enthusiasm. While I'll cover this in more depth in the next chapter, the more your employees see that you are excited about the goals, the more likely they are to become excited as well.

SMART GOALS

Over the past several years, the process of goal-setting has been neatly wrapped up in the acronym SMART:

Specific
Measurable
Achievable
Relevant
Time-bound

With the preceding material in mind, consider how the following questions help you shape your goals:

Specific
- Precisely what do you want to accomplish?
- To what extent do you control the results?
- Is the goal really easy, easy, hard, really hard, or impossible?
- Is this an outcome goal, a learning goal, or a process goal?

Measurable
- How will you know how far you've come?
- How will you know how much more there is to do?
- How will you know when you get there?
- How will you know if something is going wrong?

Achievable
- How big is your goal?
- How long will it take to accomplish your goal?
- What resources do you need to accomplish your goal?
- How will you obtain any skills and knowledge you need?
- Who will help you accomplish your goal?
- What steps are necessary to accomplish your goal?

Relevant
- Do you care?
- Do you believe you can accomplish your goal?
- How much do you want to accomplish your goal?
- Is this your goal or someone else's goal?
- What will be different if you accomplish your goal?

Time-Bound
- When will you complete your goal?
- When will you work toward your goal?
- If your goal is big, how will you break it into pieces?
- How will you know which pieces to work on?

HOW DO YOU MAINTAIN MOMENTUM?

Maintaining momentum on goals can be difficult. Fortunately, there are some techniques you can use to keep your enthusiasm and momentum going.

Make a point of celebrating successes. This doesn't mean breaking out the champagne each time you take a step, but it does mean recognizing and acknowledging your progress. The more we can see ourselves making progress, the easier it is to keep going.

Periodically review your progress and see how far you've come. While pilots may care more about the runway ahead than the runway behind them, the rest of us are motivated more by what we've accomplished than by what we have yet to do. Reviewing our accomplishments and progress increases our belief in our ability to tackle the challenges ahead of us.

Try to keep the difficulty of goals at a level where you are not overwhelmed, but do have to fully engage with the work. When a goal is overwhelming, keep decomposing it until you find a piece you can do. The more goals force you to fully engage, the more you'll enjoy the process. I'll discuss this piece in more depth below.

Finally, don't view setbacks as failures. Setbacks are simply another form of feedback. They alert you to an area of weakness or warn you of a lack of resources, knowledge, or skills. Setbacks are not an occasion to blame, but an opportunity to analyze and adjust your progress.

I'll go into this in more detail when we discuss motivation.

WHAT ABOUT SETTING GROUP GOALS?

In today's workplace, most nontrivial projects are too big for a single person to accomplish. A team is necessary. An effective team will have a clear picture of what the group is trying to accomplish and will develop ways of working together in order to accomplish their goals. This seems quite simple and obvious, yet teams constantly suffer from goal confusion: some people don't understand the goals, some are not committed to the team goals, and some are not happy with their roles. Worst of all, when asked if they understand, most people simply nod their heads. There are several factors that play into goal confusion on teams, and I will discuss most of them in Chapter 6. However, there are a few concepts around goal-setting that are important to start thinking about now.

There is an old parable about a poor village that decided to have a huge celebration. Each person was asked to bring one cup of wine and pour it into a barrel so that at the celebration everyone could get something to drink. One person decided to just pour in a cup of water since who would notice one cup of water in a large barrel of wine? Of course, when the barrel is opened, it turns out to be full of water.

Everyone has personal goals. People take jobs for their reasons, not for your reasons. When there is a conflict between personal goals and group goals, personal goals will win roughly 95 percent of the time. For group goals to be accepted, they have to be aligned with personal goals. That means connecting the goals of the team to the personal goals and aspirations of the team members.

That's where the art of goal-setting comes in. You have to paint a picture that connects the dots without making threats. This can cause some major headaches, as everyone argues about whether or not each step forward will actually get you to where you want to be. Worse, everyone just nods and then starts arguing weeks later when you thought everything was settled.

Fortunately, there is another approach.

Reverse Goal-Chaining

In reverse goal-chaining, you start by focusing on the end point. What is the ultimate outcome goal that you're trying to accomplish? Get everyone to agree that that end point is a desirable place to be.

Take a step back. Identify a subgoal that would come about very near to the final goal state. Identify as well what you need to accomplish to move from that subgoal to the final goal. Build agreement that if you were at that subgoal state, everyone would be willing to take that last step to the goal.

Then repeat this process, working backward, until you get to where you are now.

You'll notice that at no point in this process have you asked anyone to make a commitment to anything. It's all still hypothetical. However, you are generating a series of "yeses." You are also getting conceptual agreement in each stage of the process and giving people a chance to think about how much they want to get to that end state.

Only when you get to that final step where you connect the hypothetical to your actual starting point do you ask for commitment. Since they've already agreed, in concept at least, to every other step, and since you and they have had time to connect their personal goals to the final goal of the team, getting commitment on the first step is often all you need to get commitment all the way through.

I'll expand on this concept in the next chapter.

HOW DO GOALS DEFINE THE COMPANY?

To a very great extent, the goals of your company define your company. Generic goals create a generic company. How many unique law firms have you ever heard of? Vague goals create an unfocused company. Bold, aggressive goals create a bold, aggressive company.

Let's go back to culture for a moment. Recall that your culture is the encapsulated knowledge, wisdom, and experience of your organization. It's your organizational DNA. The goals that you set early on will determine how bold your culture is, how passive it is, how much it is willing to allow risk, and so forth. The potential ramifications are immense. The bigger the organization, the more powerful the goal effects will be.

Consider that when John F. Kennedy set the goal of landing a man on the moon by the end of the 1960s, he was setting a unique, bold, ambitious, extremely difficult outcome goal. That goal had a major role in defining America during that decade: it shaped our technology, it shaped our educational system, it shaped entertainment, it even shaped what we drank for breakfast. We had space pens, freeze-dried space food, and, of course, Tang.

On the entertainment front, the original "Star Trek" was a product of the space program. "Star Trek" went on the air at a time when the Apollo rockets were being launched. It rode the excitement of the space program, promising us that not only would we succeed in getting to the moon, we'd get a whole lot farther than that. On July 20, 1969, Neil Armstrong set foot on the moon. The excitement died down, and the original "Star Trek" had its last season.

While most of us will never be setting goals for an organization as large as the United States, the principle holds whether you're running a small club or a giant corporation, a school, a church, a synagogue, a for-profit entity or a nonprofit entity. Your goals will define you. They will become part of your culture, and your culture will shape your future goals.

Just because you have a well-constructed goal doesn't mean that goal is worth achieving. The biggest benefit of goals is that you might achieve them. The biggest problem with goals is that you might achieve them. If your goals are too cautious, you doom yourself to mediocrity: for instance, if your goal is to grow sales by 15 percent, that's great if you succeed. But how will you know that you shouldn't have grown by 25 percent? Of course, one answer is to set appropriate process and learning goals that will help you create the appropriate outcome goals.

THE HIGH-PERFORMANCE CYCLE

The high-performance cycle (HPC) is a phenomenon identified by Gary Latham and Edwin Locke of goal-setting fame. Essentially, it explains how goal-setting triggers a virtuous cycle of increasing performance in an organization.

Simply put, accomplishing goals leads to rewards, be those rewards financial, recognition, personal satisfaction, increased self-efficacy, and so forth. Some sort of acknowledgment is critical, though. Rewards and success at accomplishing goals lead to job satisfaction. Increased job satisfaction leads to a greater commitment to the values and beliefs of the organization. That commitment leads to increased goal relevance and a willingness to take on steadily more challenging goals. Remember, goals must be relevant in order for people to fully commit to them. If there is no relevance, performance will suffer.

We'll discuss how to jump-start the cycle in the next chapter.

GOALS AND FLOW

To a very great extent, the difficulty of a goal is a good predictor of how much someone benefits from accomplishing that goal. Accomplishing more difficult goals leads to greater confidence and self-efficacy than accomplishing easy goals. If goals are too easy, you're likely to get bored and not work as hard. On the flip side, if goals are too hard, fear of failure can become so great as to completely impair performance. Note that decomposing outcome goals into strategy-based learning and process goals can help avoid that problem.

Basically, goals work best when people set process and learning goals that make them stretch. Difficult outcome goals must be broken down so that you can focus on the parts that you can control. Remember that outcome goals provide you with the least feedback.

There is an interesting thing that happens when you are working toward a goal that forces you to stretch, is well-defined, and provides consistent feedback. It is possible then to enter a "flow" state. Flow is a concept originally defined by Mihaly Csikszentmihalyi, a psychology professor at the Peter F. Drucker School of Management at Claremont University, in his book, *Flow: The Psychology of Optimal Experience*. A flow state is one in which you are fully absorbed in what you are doing. There is no room for anything else to get in the way. Flow states are both highly productive and extremely enjoyable. When your employees are experiencing flow, they will work harder and will be excited about coming into work the next day. Just imagine the workforce you would have if you could achieve that.

It's up to you and the goals you set.

A FINAL WORD ON GOAL-SETTING

I am often told that there's no point in setting goals because the situation changes too frequently to plan effectively.

While no battle plan survives contact with the enemy, having a battle plan lets you know when things are going wrong and when they are going right. If nothing else, you know how and when to spend your resources. It's amazing how much more productive you can be when you're not fixing things that are working and missing the problems that are taking shape under your nose.

Review Quiz

1. **Goals are helpful because**
   a. They reduce distractibility
   b. Increase energy
   c. Improve persistence
   d. Focus your attention
   e. All of the above
2. **The best predictor of goal accomplishment is**
   a. A large salary
   b. A Macintosh computer
   c. Increased self-efficacy
   d. Fear of failure
   e. The risk of being fired if you fail
3. **"Do your best" is**
   a. Vague
   b. Highly idiosyncratic
   c. Extremely motivating
   d. a & b
   e. a, b, & c
4. **Goals are**
   a. Personally important
   b. Time delimited in some way
   c. Measureable

    d. Provide feedback on your progress

    e. All of the above

5. Some different types of goals are

    a. Outcome goals

    b. Process or task goals

    c. Learning goals

    d. a & c

    e. a, b, & c

6. Implementation intentions

    a. Specify when, where, and how a goal is to be obtained

    b. Can reduce distractions

    c. Require hours of rehearsal and practice

    d. a & b

    e. a & c

3

MAKING PEOPLE CARE—BEFORE YOU START

Who cares about your product? Why should anyone care? No matter how exciting, no matter how earth-shattering your idea may seem to you, odds are no one else will see it that way unless you can get them excited. Which is, of course, why you immediately should go forth and write your business plan, right? Well, maybe not.

The business plan is simply not all that interesting a document. It sounds very impressive and can make a wonderful doorstop, but it doesn't get people excited about the company. Investors, it turns out, want to see excitement. So do your employees. They'll do their jobs if they're paid, but they'll only make that extra effort, that push that gets them coming in early, staying late, or working weekends, if they deeply and passionately care about the company.

Alex Pentland, a professor at MIT, conducted a very interesting experiment on the power of excitement and enthusiasm. He took one group of businesspeople and one group of investors. The investors were given only a set of business plans for several prospective start-up companies. The businesspeople were given both the business plans and a live pitch. Even after controlling for the fact that the two types of groups might have completely different ideas about what companies would be viable, the two groups made completely different choices of which plans to fund. Pentland was able to determine ahead of time which plans the executives would pick by measuring their excitement and enthusiam.

Whether you're a small business owner, the founder of a start-up company, or a manager in a large firm, if people don't care, you're not going to make much progress. Granted, if you offer enough money or other incentives, you can always hire people to work on your product. If they're not excited, however, you're going to spend all your time pushing them, and if they get a better offer, they'll be gone in a heartbeat. Mercenaries are not known for their loyalty. If the news reports about the contractors the U.S. government hired to guard our embassy in Kabul are any indication, mercenaries are not much known for their decorum or concern for the hiring agency either.

CREATE EXCITEMENT IF YOU WANT ENTHUSIASM

Unfortunately, what I see in most of the businesses I work with is a reliance on bonuses, rewards, prizes, and similar incentives, as though producing the product was a carnival game: make four sales and win a stuffed animal. Sink three bugs in the software and get the grand prize! Even worse, some companies award prizes to people on a team for outdoing other members of the team. It may come as a shock to some managers, but this is not the way to get people to care about the company. It is, however, a good way to get people to care about the competition—no, not the companies you are competing with. Rather, your employees become focused on competing with one another. Unfortunately, when members of a team are competing with one another, even for fun, they are working to maximize their own rewards, not maximize the company's results, a topic we'll cover in more detail in subsequent chapters. For now, the important point is that we're back to the carnival mentality.

Now some carnival games can certainly be fun, and they do get people to come play. They also see people walk away when they get bored, if they find the game too hard, or if they win a few times. Is that really what you want to have happen in your company? Are you looking for people who are after a momentary thrill or will leave as soon as the going gets tough? Are you really after employees who leave as soon as they've collected a few bonuses? Taking this one step further, do you really want clients who view you as a commodity?

The fact is, if your employees view you solely as a commodity that satisfies their needs for income, don't expect that your customers are going to see you any differently. If you can't get the people who are building your product to care or be excited, how will you manage with customers who have a marketplace full of products to choose from?

Let's look at this another way: would you rather hire someone who appears disinterested and hope they became enthusiastic later, or would you rather hire someone who is enthusiastic at the job interview? Even better, wouldn't you like to hire the person who becomes visibly excited when you tell him what you're trying to do? The fact is, enthusiasm sells. If your employees are excited, it will show in the quality of their work, and that will help distinguish your product on the market. If your employees are excited, they'll talk, blog, and tweet about you. They will be personally invested in the company in a way that stock options and bonuses can support but cannot create.

CAN YOU SAY WHAT YOU SEE?

Sadly, one of the things that I've noticed when working with different businesses is that very few people can answer the question "What are you trying to accomplish?" Certainly they can talk about products that they want to build or milestones that they want to achieve, but very rarely can anyone talk about how the company's product will make a difference or somehow change the world. In short, if the company has a vision of what it's doing and where it's going, few people are able to articulate that vision. Given finite resources, a vision is the first step toward determining where to focus those resources.

Scott Adams's *Dilbert* aptly pokes fun at the vague, vacuous, and all too self-important visions developed by so many organizations. Despite what Dilbert might say, a well-crafted vision represents a stake in the ground, an opportunity to develop a shared sense of where the organization is going. After all, if you don't know where you're going, you can waste a lot of energy not getting there. If there is disagreement among the leaders of the organization on the vision, that disagreement will translate into confusion among the membership, reduced ability to plan for the future, and an increased difficulty in deciding the best course of action.

When employees don't know the vision, setting individual and team goals becomes increasingly difficult. Goals appear disconnected or lack focus. Employees may not see the point of certain decisions or of goals assigned to them, leading to decreased motivation. More to the point, if employees don't know what the vision is, they won't care deeply about the company.

Remember the high-performance cycle from the previous chapter? Employees who are happy and satisfied in their jobs will be committed to the goals of the company and willing to take on the tough challenges. The satisfaction gained from successfully meeting those challenges, and the rewards given by the company, will increase their overall satisfaction and happiness, leading to increased commitment to the company and its goals. Unfortunately, this does not happen very often. There are many reasons why the cycle fails, which will be addressed in subsequent chapters. Initially, though, the cycle often fails before it can even get started: it fails when there is no vision.

The company's vision is what jump-starts the high-performance cycle. The vision is what excites employees in the first place, before there is any job satisfaction, before there are rewards, before there are goals. The vision is a key part of what gets your prospects to accept a job at your company in the first place, and it's what gets them committed and convinced that the project is worth that extra push, those late nights or long weekends.

Everyone wants money, but it doesn't excite people.

Fundamentally, "make lots of money" is not a vision. It's a dream, a very fine dream, but a dream. It's a dream that a company can turn into reality by living up to and realizing its vision. Oddly enough, while making lots of money is certainly important to people and certainly something that many people would happily have happen, it actually does not excite people all that much, and it certainly won't excite your prospective clients. After all, if your vision is to make a lot of money, what does that say about the role your customers will play in that vision? Do you really think they are going to be excited about making you rich? As for your employees, if you make money the issue, they know that someone in the company is going to get a lot more than they will. That tends to dampen the excitement more than a little.

Now this may seem somewhat odd. Why isn't money exciting? After all, if a business does not make money, it does not stay in business. Making money is certainly highly important, but it very quickly loses its motivational value. But, as managers frequently ask, why not offer the money and tell your employees you'll fire them if they don't put in those extra hours? Carrot and stick, isn't that really all that's needed?

Well, no. Slaves are not known for their innovation, their excitement, or their commitment to quality. The more you have to push people, the less you'll get for your efforts.

WHAT IS A VISION?

The traditional definition of a vision in business is a statement about the desires, beliefs, hopes, and aspirations of the company. It should be realistic, challenging, and attainable, and it should flow naturally from your values as an organization.

What does it mean? Fundamentally, it means that in a few short sentences, you need to evoke an image in people's minds that will get them to sit up and take notice. The vision also has to make sense for your company. A vision that does not fit with what your company does will only make you look silly. A vision that does not match with your organizational culture will not be believed. A vision that aggressively tells people how your company will change the world will get attention. It needs to answer a few very basic questions:

- Who are we?
- Where are we going? How will the world be different, even if in only a small way, if we're successful?
- Why do we care? Does our vision inspire the current members of our organization to believe in and be willing to work toward it?
- Why does anyone else care? How will our vision inspire people to join the business and work to bring the vision to fruition? How will our vision tell our potential customers that supporting our products is in their best interest?
- How will we know if we're making progress? How will we know when we get there?

Blaise Pascal once said, "I didn't have time to write you a short letter, so I wrote you a long one." A vision should be short; if it takes more than five minutes to convey, you've lost your audience.

Answering these questions is not necessarily easy. For an established organization, the leadership may not always share the same vision. Even in a new venture, the founders may not always see things the same way. Allowing the vision to fragment serves nobody: fragmented vision means fragmented focus. I once interviewed several board members of one company whose different visions had only a single point of agreement: that they did not want to go out of business. It was no wonder the company was stagnating. The board members all had completely different perspectives and spent their time talking past one another. One person's initiative was another person's distraction.

A key element of making a vision work for any organization is making sure that all the significant stakeholders feel that they are involved in the process. If people feel excluded, it's harder to sell the vision to them later, and they are less likely to commit to bringing it to reality. The more people who need to be included in forging the vision, the more challenging it can be. Honing down and bringing together the disparate views of multiple people is an iterative process.

That means starting with a small group, maybe only a couple of people, maybe only the CEO. It can be hard, though, with only one person; it's much easier to create a vision when you have someone to bounce ideas off of. Brainstorm what the world will look like if the company is successful; let the questions guide you, but imagine the world. Most companies never really pursue this step. Their leaders might imagine a successful product, but they don't think about what that really means. What will have to happen? What are the consequences of the product's success? What opportunities does that success create?

As the vision starts to take shape, bring in additional people. Get their input, but don't lose control of the vision. Find out what they think, what excites and what doesn't excite them. Weave their contributions into the overall picture. You will probably find that it's starting to look like a big jigsaw puzzle. That's OK. Play with the pieces, experiment, explore the vision. Don't try to force it to happen in a single marathon session; rather, spend a few days or even a few weeks at it. The vision is important. Treat it that way.

Only once your vision has started to develop a coherent shape should you work on boiling it down into a few short, vivid sentences. The key word here is *vivid*. To show you what I mean, the vision statement of a certain financial company is, "The Big Financial Company will be a provider of customer-focused, value-added financial and human resources services, delivered in an efficient, competent, and consultative manner."

Still awake? This is a vision statement that fails in almost every way. To begin with, it's seriously boring. Who is going to be excited about customer-focused, efficient deliveries? How does this vision tell anyone that the world will be different? Why would potential clients come to TBFC instead of one of its competitors? Does this seriously distinguish it from the competition? Furthermore, how will anyone know if this vision comes true? The vision does not have wide appeal; indeed, if it appeals to anyone, it's probably senior management. And they are certainly a very small minority. The vision needs to appeal to a great many more people than just a few diehards. I'm not completely certain, but I believe this vision statement was written by cartoonist Scott Adams, of *Dilbert* fame.

HOW DO THE VISION AND THE GOALS INTERACT?

Once you have a clear vision, then you can start building out goals to bring it to life. Remember what we discussed about goal-setting. The key to successful goals is making them as specific as possible. You must know where you want to go before you make plans on how to get there. Also, by having specific, clear goals and a clear destination, you'll be better able to set deadlines for each step; this lets you know how much progress you're making, alerts you early if something isn't working, and makes planning much, much easier. The Big Financial Company's vision is so vague that it's virtually impossible to come up with goals that would bring it to life. How would you measure success? For that matter, how will you know if you're successful? If you have to engage in complex gymnastics in order to figure out the goals, odds are you have a problem with the vision.

A vivid vision means that you can work backward from there to where you are now. Recall our discussion of reverse goal-chaining. Oddly enough, when you're trying to figure out how to get from one place to another, it's much more effective to work backward from a destination than it is to work forward from a starting point. Once you have people buying into the destination, then you can define a point a short distance from that destination. Once you've identified that point near your destination, you can easily obtain buy-in that if you were at that point, you could step to the end. Working backward means that you are creating implicit buy-in every step of the way so that when it's time to get started, everyone is convinced and ready to go. If you work forward, you have to spend your time and energy arguing each step.

CRAFTING YOUR VISION

One board of directors told me that their vision of the future was that their company "would still be in business in five years."

Avoiding failure, while worthwhile, is not a particularly effective vision. This board in question cannot commit to long-term plans nor agree on how to apply resources and rarely follows through on those plans it does eventually commit to. There is no agreement on the board as to where the organization is going.

What will help you paint that vivid future image for your company?

Twenty-Twenty and Astigmatism

Microsoft's early vision was "A PC on every desk and in every home." While there are certainly remote corners of the world where there are no PCs, Microsoft's vision has effectively become a reality. Along the way, it had some very easy metrics for tracking its vision. That focused its resources and made it one of the most successful businesses in history. Its vision defined Microsoft, told its employees and everyone else where it was going, stated how the world would be different when it got there, and inspired people to care, and progress was easy to track. Microsoft knew what it was trying to accomplish. As PC sales continued to grow throughout the 1990s, the excitement was palpable.

Today, Microsoft's vision is "To help people and businesses throughout the world realize their full potential."

What does that mean? How can they tell if they are making progress? Every data point must be analyzed, debated, discussed, and interpreted. By the time that's done, there's not a whole lot of clarity, to say nothing of excitement, left. What if the best way of accomplishing Microsoft's vision was to encourage everyone to buy an Apple? There is simply no reason to care about Microsoft's brave new world. As a clear destination, it is somewhat lacking. It could have been written by Dilbert's pointy-haired boss.

By way of comparison, Google's vision "is to organize the world's information and make it universally accessible and useful." This is remarkably similar to Microsoft's original vision, in that it is short, clear, and measurable. It also answers the "vision" questions listed at the beginning of this chapter:

- It defines Google: a company that finds and organizes information.
- It tells everyone where Google is going and how it will know when it gets there: toward a world where information is organized and available.

- It clearly states how the world will be different when it got there: information that is scattered and disorganized today will be available and easily accessible tomorrow.
- It asserts why Google and everyone else cares: information is the lifeblood of the modern economy. The more information is available and the more easily it can be accessed, the easier it is for businesses and individuals to accomplish their goals.
- It provides benchmarks for assessing progress: each new advance in search functionality, each new initiative to bring information online, moves them closer in a clear and measurable fashion.

Now that is quite a bit different from Microsoft's current vision. Not only can we imagine what that world looks like, we can experience a taste of it every time we sit down at a computer and open a browser. It's already hard to imagine what it was like finding information on a topic in the dark ages, better known as the pre-Google days of the 1990s. My five-year-old son tells me to "ask Google" whenever I don't know the answer to a question. Google is exciting, and a big part of why it is exciting is that we benefit from its success. Its leaders successfully created something that makes its employees, its clients, and even its competitors care.

Making Your Vision Inclusive

A characteristic of a good vision is that it is inclusive. It draws people in and shows them how they are going to benefit. Both Microsoft's original vision and Google's current vision do that very well. It's implicit, but it's there. Microsoft's current vision of helping us all achieve our full potential is, paradoxically, not so inclusive. It feels like something they are going to do *to* us. Maybe it's because it is so hard to know what our full potential is, or maybe it's because, unless you happen to be one of those people with infinite time and money, achieving potential in one area usually means not achieving it somewhere else. Most of us have made choices in our lives that have led to our focusing our time and energy in one field instead of another, on family instead of a hobby, for example.

Another important way in which a vision is inclusive is that it clearly illustrates that the risks and the sacrifices necessary to bring that vision to life will be shared. Failure is failure for everyone, from the highest to the lowest, just as success is success for everyone.

At one start-up I worked for a good many years ago, we were facing a critical deadline. Our CEO walked into the engineering team meeting to give us a pep talk. He spoke for several minutes on the importance of hitting our deadline, of how much he had faith that we would work as long and as hard as necessary to get the job done. He ended by telling us just how much he was looking forward to seeing the product working after he got back from his monthlong vacation in Hawaii. One of the VPs, who had apparently not been warned ahead of time that the CEO was going away, almost choked on his coffee.

There were several problems with this little talk. It was not about the customers. It was not about how important it was to get the product to market because of the difference it would make to the users. Instead, the speech was all about him and what we had to do to serve his and the company's needs. The final bit at the end merely illustrated the degree of disconnect and the extent to which he felt that he was entitled to reap the rewards without making any of the sacrifices. When he got back, at least one person had quit, the rest were up in arms, and the product was not working.

Perhaps one of the most famous examples of communicating an inclusive vision is Winston Churchill's famous "blood, toil, tears, and sweat" speech given at the eve of Britain's entrance into World War II. Churchill connects with the listeners by showing that he knows and understands the suffering they will have to endure: "I have nothing to offer but blood, toil, tears, and sweat. We have before us an ordeal of the most grievous kind. We have before us many, many months of struggle and suffering."

His phraseology includes himself. In other words, the British people are not suffering alone while the leaders are comfortable. Everyone is struggling, everyone is suffering. The blood, toil, tears, and sweat will come from all the people, from the lowest to the highest.

He then follows that statement with clear and unmistakable long-term goals and intentions:

> You ask, what is our policy? I say it is to wage war by land, sea, and air. War with all our might and with all the strength God has given us, and to wage war against a monstrous tyranny never surpassed in the dark and lamentable catalogue of human crime. That is our policy.
>
> You ask, what is our aim? I can answer in one word. It is victory. Victory at all costs—victory in spite of all terrors—victory, however long and hard the road may be, for without victory there is no survival.

Let that be realized. No survival for the British Empire, no survival for all that the British Empire has stood for, no survival for the urge, the impulse of the ages, that mankind shall move forward toward his goal.

Throughout his speech, Churchill makes it clear that he is fighting not for the glory of Winston Churchill, not just for the survival of the British Empire, but for the values and aspirations that the Empire stands for. In a sense, he is initiating change by unfreezing the current situation by highlighting the threat that exists to the country if action is not taken, a point we discussed in Chapter 1. His goals are lofty goals indeed and certainly goals that can provide meaning and purpose to any life.

Now, let me be clear: you don't have to be one of the greatest leaders in modern history to make a stirring speech. You don't have to be fighting Nazi Germany to convince people that your cause is worth fighting for. You don't have to give purpose to people's entire lives.

What you must do is create a powerful, inclusive vision and then get the message out.

COMMUNICATING YOUR VISION

Having a vision is a good start. After all, if you don't have anything to communicate, then all the communication skills in the world won't help you. The first, and most important, element of effective communications is having something to communicate.

The second is being able to communicate it well.

We have arrived at one of those areas where countless people run into trouble. It doesn't matter whether you're a CEO, senior VP, frontline manager, head of a nonprofit, clergy, teacher, or anyone else who needs to communicate with others. To be fair, clergy and teachers usually do better only because they have to get up in front of people all the time; however, even in schools, churches, and synagogues, I've observed plenty of people who are excellent speakers from a content perspective who still cannot communicate the essential elements of their vision.

The key to effectively communicating your vision is letting your enthusiasm show. Unfortunately, too many people have been steeped in the belief that "this is a business" and "we are logical, rational professionals."

While we like to think of ourselves as rational, the fact is, we're just not that good at being rational. Logic is fine, it's valuable, but it's not everything. Fans of "Star Trek" will recall that Mr. Spock is often puzzled by how dramatically his logic fails to motivate others. While logic is important, we use emotion to determine how much attention and credence to give to what we hear.

If this doesn't make sense, let me put it this way: If you don't seem enthusiastic about the vision, why should your employees be? If you don't seem to care about the vision, why should anyone else? If you aren't moved by it, why should anyone else be? If you aren't willing to put in the effort to make the vision reality, why would anyone else? In the end, you cannot threaten people into bringing a vision to life. You can get them involved, get them excited, and then get out of their way.

That means showing your excitement and enthusiasm when you talk about the vision. It means being animated and energetic. If you stand in front of people and are completely still when you speak, they're going to take that as lack of enthusiasm on your part. That doesn't mean that you have to pace up and down, but it does mean that your body language, tone of voice, and cadence must express your excitement.

I've often heard it said that most people would rather be the person in the coffin than the one standing in front of everyone delivering the eulogy. If you truly can't bring yourself to stand in front of others and give a dynamic talk, then pick someone else as your spokesman or hire someone who can deliver it. The higher up you are in the company, the better it is if you are the one communicating the vision. If you really can't do that, then it's better to have the message delivered by someone who can. Just make sure that you're there backing him or her up with your presence and your approval.

VISION AND FLOW

Recall that in the last chapter I discussed the concept of flow: an extremely pleasurable state in which someone is so deeply engaged in a task that she is oblivious to anything else. As I mentioned, the more your employees experience flow, the happier and more enthusiastic they'll be about coming to work each day.

Your company's vision is a tool for increasing the likelihood that people will experience a flow state. When you present people with an exciting, worthy vision that taps into their own hopes, dreams, and goals, you are helping them to make the vision personally relevant. The more personally relevant it is, the more they will commit to making it a reality.

Your goal is to make it easy for them to buy in, to connect to something bigger than they are, and to personally care about bringing that something to life. The more they care, the more they will enjoy the process, the harder they'll work, and the more willing they will be to put up with the inevitable frustrations and sacrifices along the way.

A number of years ago, I attended a Boot Camp for Start-Ups conference. At the end of the talk on "Giving Your Elevator Pitch," three volunteers from the audience were given the opportunity to stand up in front of the several hundred people in the room and give a thirty-second pitch on a well-known company that the presenter would name.

I was one of the three volunteers, and I drew Amazon.com (the other two companies were Palm and eBay). My prep time was the time it took me to jog from the back of the auditorium where I was sitting to the podium.

I gave my thirty-second pitch and returned to my seat to enthusiastic applause. The person sitting next to me turned as I sat down and said, "You made it feel like it would be a personal tragedy for *me* if Amazon didn't exist!"

That's the idea.

Review Quiz

1. **The high-performance cycle**
   a. Is what Lance Armstrong rides
   b. Connects job satisfaction to commitment to goals to rewards to job satisfaction
   c. Says that performance is driven by increasing salaries
   d. Is a method of driving performance through error reduction
   e. Is a process of continuous improvement by eliminating the weakest performers
2. **An effective means of motivation is**
   a. Large raises and bonuses
   b. Your own excitement
   c. Prizes
   d. Competition between team members
   e. All of the above

3. Why is a clear vision important?
    a. It helps bring clarity and meaning to goals.
    b. It helps the company impress customers.
    c. It means that you don't need glasses.
    d. It prevents people from caring too much.
    e. None of the above

4. A question that a vision needs to answer is
    a. Who are we?
    b. Why do we care?
    c. Why does anyone else care?
    d. How will our actions change the world, even if only a little bit?
    e. All of the above

5. A vision
    a. Springs forth fully formed like Athena from the brow of Zeus
    b. Must be long and detailed
    c. Should be short and vivid
    d. Never changes
    e. Only involves the executive staff

6. A vision is inclusive when it
    a. Tells people what you'll do to them
    b. Shows people that risk and sacrifice will be shared
    c. Only focuses on the clients or customers
    d. Focuses on making money
    e. All of the above

7. The first step to communicating effectively is to
    a. Wear a blue suit and tie
    b. Stand in the spotlight
    c. Walk up and down the stage
    d. Speak loudly
    e. Have something to say

8. Before you can communicate your vision, you must
    a. Understand why your vision inspires you
    b. Understand why you care about your vision
    c. Be aware of your own hopes, dreams, and aspirations
    d. Be willing to let people see how much the vision matters to you
    e. All of the above

4

BUILDING THE FOUNDATION: WHOM, AND HOW, DO YOU HIRE?

F iguring out exactly who you need to hire means more than just throwing some terms down on paper. Buzzwords are easy, and requiring some number of years of experience feels good but doesn't necessarily get you what you need. Hiring is about understanding your objectives and finding people who can bring those objectives to life. An early focus on specific skills limits the number of available solutions.

Conversely, there are times when specific skills are vital and really would take too long to learn on the job. The trick is to find the balance and identify what you really need. For example, you would not want to hire a brain surgeon if you weren't completely certain about his ability to perform operations, nor would you want to hire a pilot if you had doubts about her ability to fly. In these situations, the opportunity costs of continuing the job search are lower than the costs of hiring the wrong person.

In most jobs, though, the opportunity costs of keeping the job search open arbitrarily long are much greater than the cost of hiring someone not perfect. Despite this, I've seen business after business spend many months looking for that perfect candidate when they could have hired a qualified person after one month who could have been up to speed in another month or two. The cost in work not being accomplished is often far greater than the cost in paying someone to learn on the job.

CALLING DR. STAFF!

It is futile to search for the candidate who will solve all your problems. Some years ago I was sitting in a product design meeting. The discussion kept circling around some particularly knotty issues. Someone finally commented that we'd have to make sure to hire someone with the particular expertise in question, and in one fell swoop, that issue was assigned to a nonexistent future employee. This was not necessarily a problem . . . yet. It became a problem, however, as the meeting progressed:

> "We don't have anyone on the team who can handle [technology] either."
> "That'll be the next hire."
> "Wasn't the next hire supposed to be [original problem]?"
> "We'll need someone who can do both."

So it went, each problem being assigned to the same nonexistent person. Unfortunately, each individual present had a very different idea of what that person looked like. College catalogs often list a vast number of courses in a wide range of subjects taught by "Staff." By the end of that meeting, Dr. Staff was the only person who could have handled the job. Unfortunately, searching for a candidate who is a world-renowned expert in everything tends to be very frustrating. Dropping the "world-renowned" doesn't necessarily help either.

Before you can start hiring people, or even start looking, you need to know whom you are looking for and how you'll recognize that candidate: effective goal-setting includes recognizing success. If your outcome goal is to hire "qualified" people, then you may not know what you're looking for until after the fact. If your process goals are to identify what sort of people you need and learn how to find them and recruit them, then you can accomplish your outcome goal of hiring qualified people because you know ahead of time what "qualified" means. The second set of goals—the process goals—require more upfront effort but are more effective.

When you know whom you're looking for, you're also more likely to get the best candidate instead of the best interviewee. It's easy for people to Google "job interview" and find out dozens of possible interview questions and answers. Remember, people wear suits to interviews in order to make a good impression. There really is an element of theater to the interviewing process. Don't get fooled by the special effects.

HOW DO YOU KNOW WHAT TO LOOK FOR?

The field of organizational psychology talks a great deal about job analysis. Job analysis focuses primarily on breaking jobs down into specific tasks that make up the job or into specific worker behaviors that, in theory, make up the job. In addition to being time-consuming and potentially expensive, traditional job-analysis techniques are of limited use in many of the nontraditional jobs of today. Still, job analysis teaches some important lessons and gives us a place to start.

Jobs can be broken down into hard skills, soft skills, behaviors, and goals:

•   **Hard skills** are those domain-specific skills that a candidate absolutely must have in order to be qualified for the job. A heart surgeon needs one set of skills; a computer programmer needs another. Identifying hard skills can be surprisingly difficult. I see companies looking for software engineers with specific programming language experience when the hard skill in question is the ability to program. The specific language is merely a manifestation of that skill.

•   **Soft skills** are those non-domain-specific skills that are critical to functioning on the job. They include the ability to work as part of a team, problem solving, ability to learn on the job, personal responsibility, self-discipline, communicating with others, adaptability, and so forth. These are often more critical than the hard skills yet are also the least well understood. The hotshot programmer who ignored the rest of the team in every previous job isn't likely to change just for you.

•   **Behaviors** are those actions that an ideal job candidate would have exhibited in previous jobs. These might include neatness, punctuality, or courtesy. Behaviors are important when they contribute to goal accomplishment but may be a distraction otherwise. For example, many technology companies are quite comfortable with employees who work odd hours so long as they get the job done. Some organizations encourage a very direct, argumentative style, while others want to see a mellow, more courteous debate. Neither is necessarily right or wrong; it depends on the organization.

  • **Goals** are the expected results of the new hire, or what you expect the candidate to accomplish. From a hiring perspective, it's most helpful to focus on the outcome goals. It's more important to understand what you want someone to accomplish than to get bogged down in the details of how he will accomplish it, especially before you've actually hired him.

Note that there is a certain degree of overlap among the various categories: sometimes knowledge of a specific programming language may be legitimately considered a hard skill even though much of the time it's more of a soft skill. Sometimes you really need someone who can accomplish a result in a very specific way, while other times you need someone who is good at getting things done. Ultimately, these categories should be used as guidelines. The job-analysis police will not break down your door if you fiddle with them. Adjust if you're not getting the results you want.

Next, how do you know which skills, and other requirements, are needed for a job? For that you have to do some research. The answers will vary according to your organization and the specific job. You need to find subject matter experts, who can include the following:

  • Other people doing the same or a similar job
  • Managers of people doing that job
  • People who used to do that job or a similar job

The first is far and away the best source of information. Get information from more than one person, though, to help weed out idiosyncratic approaches.

Managers are not a bad choice but often tend to focus more on behaviors that they want to see rather than behaviors that are actually critical to the job. I find, for example, that many managers would rather see someone working forty hours than someone who is working an indeterminate number of hours but who regularly gets the job done. Hours are only important when there is a direct and measurable correlation between hours and results.

People who used to do the job are another source of information, although how valuable that information is often depends on how long it's been since (and how well) they've done that job.

Once you've collected the information, you must put it together into a coherent picture. Think about what you're looking at, and play with the pieces. Developing a good picture of whom you need for a job is an art as much as a science. Fortunately, it doesn't need to be perfect in order to be useful. The key is to avoid crafting a set of job requirements that leave you looking for Dr. Staff.

BECOMING A TALENT MAGNET

Once you know whom to look for, you need to attract them to your company.

Recognize that no one is coming to work for you because they care about your needs. They are looking to satisfy their needs. You must demonstrate to them from the beginning that meeting your needs will also meet their needs.

Ask yourself if you are meeting the actual needs of potential applicants, the needs you wish they had, or your own needs. At this stage, you must craft your message to address the needs of your target audience and create a compelling opportunity that will attract them to your company.

Since you don't know the potential applicants, this may seem a daunting task; fortunately, there are some key elements common to almost everyone. Good job analysis will give you a strong sense of how your ideal employee rates on each factor.

• **The biggest need is safety.** People look for a job in which they will feel safe. This can mean a lot of different things. For some, it means working for a company that is too big to go out of business. For others, it means having a set of transferable skills and the opportunity to develop and hone those skills. Since many people find the job-hunting process stressful and unpleasant, part of safety usually includes "will last for a while." Communicate the safety you offer.

• **Related to safety is risk.** I am told that people don't want to take risks. Actually, many people are perfectly happy to take risks. What they dislike is unquantifiable risk. People like to feel in control and that the rewards are worth the risk. The perception of control and the belief that they understand and can manage the risks are often enough to convince people to take a chance. Make clear the risks you are asking people to take, demonstrate how you are prepared to help them manage those risks, and illustrate the potential rewards.

- **Next is growth.** Job satisfaction and the opportunity to perform a variety of tasks and learn new skills go hand-in-hand. Most people enjoy the opportunity to grow and develop in their jobs; the side effect is that they will become steadily more capable of handling increasingly difficult tasks. What growth opportunities do you offer?
- **It's not enough to do a variety of different tasks.** It's also critical that those tasks matter to the organization. It's hard to take pride in irrelevant work. Be sure to demonstrate the relevance of the job.
- **Being part of a larger organization can be extremely important and a powerful motivating factor.** The job is not just a source of money but a source of connection to other people. Are you looking for team players or individual performers? Will they be part of a bigger vision or just making money for the company? The former is far more appealing than the latter.

A key element of attracting top talent is the prestige of the company. People want to take pride in their jobs; after all, work is a huge part of their lives. Companies such as Google or IBM have prestige associated with them. Others need to create the image. Understand how people view you and tailor your message accordingly.

Your website can make a big difference. The less someone knows about you, the more your website introduces them to the company. A website that is hard to navigate, confusing, or irritating creates a certain perception of the company. In today's world, a nonexistent website is simply inexcusable and really sends the message that you can't get your act together. Forget about secrecy, stealth mode, or what have you; you need something professional looking. A clean, easy to navigate website is a powerful advertisement for you. It sets the tone and starts people off thinking positively. Perhaps paradoxically, even though most of your management team will usually be complete unknowns to the majority of job applicants, putting up their bios is helpful. It creates a sense of familiarity and trust right from the beginning.

THE GODOT EFFECT

There's a training exercise that I conduct fairly regularly focused on leadership, negotiation, and creative problem solving. Participants are given a problem and a list of people who might be able to help them, only some of whom are actually present. The objective is to figure out solutions that do not involve the missing people. What is particularly fascinating is that every time I conduct this exercise a significant number of participants become fixated on the missing people, convinced that if those people were present, all the problems would immediately evaporate. They spend the exercise waiting for help that never arrives.

When I ask at the end, "Why do you think that [missing] person will actually help you? What if he has his own agenda?" Participants are taken aback. They never considered the fact that if Godot arrives, he might have his own wants and needs. I've run this exercise with managers, college students, psychologists, engineers, and people in many other fields, and the same behaviors emerge every time. In each case, the person who is not present becomes the repository of the hopes and dreams of the rest of the group. In the end, that "person" becomes a tool whose only purpose for existing is to solve the problems of the group.

When it comes to the hiring process, the longer this behavior persists, the harder it is for the employees of an organization to find anyone they are willing to hire. First, none of the people they are looking at actually fits the mental image they've developed. To make matters worse, the longer the process lasts, the more the nonexistent hire is imbued with ever more mythical qualities. Dr. Staff is not only expected to show up eventually but to be totally and completely enthusiastic about working for the company. People who do not exhibit that mindless enthusiasm are not deemed serious candidates. To be fair, the search rarely lasts forever. Eventually, people get tired of interviewing candidates and someone does get hired. Often, though, it's the last person to walk through the door as opposed to the most qualified of the people who came through.

The more upfront time you spend understanding what you really need and how you'll recognize that person, the more confidence you'll have in your ability to decide. The more confidence you have, the less likely you are to get stuck waiting for Godot.

HOW DOES THE HIRING PROCESS SHAPE YOUR CULTURE?

The most frequent complaints I hear from managers is that their employees are unmotivated, no one will step up to the plate when there's an emergency, and people take a "that's not my job" attitude when asked to do something unusual or outside their normal duties. I used to wonder why that kept happening. After all, didn't they hire those guys?

Indeed they did. Part of the problem is that the managers often didn't know what they were actually looking for. However, even when the organization did know whom it was looking for, it still wasn't getting the right people. The problem was more subtle. It wasn't *who* they were hiring that was the source of the trouble. It was *how* they were hiring.

Remember that culture is your organization's DNA: it shapes everything you do. Unlike DNA, it is also shaped by everything you do. How a company approaches its hiring process will teach a great deal about the organizational culture and will also reinforce certain areas of that culture. How well candidates resonate with the aspects of culture expressed through the hiring process will have a strong influence on who gets hired. Bringing people in who are already tuned to particular aspects of the organizational culture will strengthen those aspects.

In short, how a company recruits will determine whether it creates a culture of aggressive problem solving or passive waiting in the face of difficulties, unexpected situations, or anything in between.

To take an extreme example, I regularly see job ads that announce a position but provide no information about the company, the product, or the management team. Many give no website or phone number and provide no physical address. Apparently they expect people to shoot résumés into a black hole. Lest you think I am making this up, I actually spoke to the CEO of one such business. She patiently explained to me that they didn't have a website because they were in stealth mode. She then indignantly told me that the engineers of today are totally unmotivated. When she asked them for résumés, they asked for a description of the job and then had the unmitigated gall to get upset when she didn't want to provide one.

A far more common example are those companies that ask for résumés and specify no phone calls, or that provide a phone number, which usually goes to voice mail. Calling risks having one's résumé tossed for being "annoying."

Still other companies will respond only to the people who aggressively make the phone calls. Those who call repeatedly are the ones who get called back and invited to interviews.

What sort of people will respond to these different approaches? The first two yield very similar results: the aggressive problem solvers get frustrated because they cannot get past the wall of silence. If they are effective at solving problems and focusing their energies, they concentrate on the businesses from which they are getting a response. Meanwhile, the people who are happy to sit back and wait do just that. The longer the business takes to make its decisions, the more likely those people are the ones still available. Even the more aggressive players have been given the very clear message that the correct behavior in this company is to shut up and wait. Thus are the seeds of culture sown.

In general, although not perfect, the company using the third approach is probably a better place to be than the companies in examples one and two. The danger is going too far in the other direction: the aggressive approach becomes the norm for interaction in all situations. Team members never really take the time to get to know one another and understand each other's working styles. They never develop trust and a strong sense of team identity, limiting overall productivity. We'll discuss that in Chapter 6.

Overall, the more cognizant you are of your cultural values and what behaviors you wish to reinforce, the more likely it is that you will hire the people who will not just provide the skills you need but also reinforce the aspects of your culture that will help make the company successful.

WHAT ARE YOU REALLY OFFERING?

If you've been paying attention to this point, you'll realize that you're not just offering someone a job. If that's all you're doing, then you're going to be competing with a lot of other companies over pay, benefits, vacation, work hours, and so forth. That's a losing game, not only because there's always someone out there with more resources, but also because you're going to lose out to the businesses that know what they are really offering.

So what are you offering? You are offering people a chance to become involved in something bigger than they are. You are offering them a chance to make a difference in some way to someone. You are offering people an opportunity to put their skills to work in an environment that will support their growth and allow them to feel pride in what they do. You are providing them status, identity, purpose, and security.

You are offering them a vision of the future. The greater your intentional control and awareness of the process, the more successful you'll be.

HOW DO YOU SELECT CANDIDATES?

After some sort of initial résumé screening, interviews are probably the most popular means of selecting candidates. Unfortunately, interviews are also the least reliable because they are the most subject to unconscious bias and manipulation. Indeed, given the increasing prevalence of interview coaching, I suspect that unstructured interviews are only going to become less reliable over time. However, of the various techniques available, interviews are also the easiest and least expensive. The biggest danger is that you get what you pay for.

Proven Applicant-Screening Techniques

Fortunately, there are a number of techniques you can use to find the right people. Let's quickly go over some of them, and then we'll look at ways to make interviewing more effective.

• **Various aptitude tests are used in some fields.** These are most effective in environments in which there is a clear agreement on what constitutes an accurate, meaningful, and useful response. The programming test that requires candidates to correctly guess which menu items would show up when the Microsoft Visual C++ compiler was in debug mode is a perfect example of what *not* to do.

• **Various forms of role-playing and simulation exercises are powerful techniques for seeing how people will act under pressure and in different scenarios.** The "virtual inbox" exercise is one in which management candidates are put in a scenario in which they are "substituting" for someone who has been unexpectedly called away. They have a fixed amount of time to work through the inbox, making decisions as they go.

• **Leaderless group discussions are often used to see how people behave in an unstructured team setting.** Does the candidate try to take control? Does she solicit ideas from others? Does she shut down discussion or encourage others? The Massachusetts School of Professional Psychology uses a variant of this as part of its admissions process.

My wife, who is an educational therapist, and I constructed a number of extremely elaborate serious game exercises designed to reveal the way people deal with unexpected problems. We found that the way the subjects generally dealt with the problems in the game mirrored how they would deal with unexpected problems in the workplace. In other words, those who gave up easily in the game did the same in the work environment. Those who looked for creative solutions in the game were more likely to do so at work as well.

It's possible to become extremely creative in screening job applicants. Periodically, go back and compare your results to the types of people you were expecting to get. Is the system working?

Keep in mind that a system that focuses on a specific skill or approach to problem solving will generate a team that has deep, but not broad, expertise: they're very good at what they're good at, but their skills fall off rapidly outside that area. A team with broad expertise is capable of handling a wider variety of problems, even if they may not be as strong in any specific area as the deep team. Teams with a wider range of problem-solving techniques are more effective over the long run.

Now, back to everyone's favorite topic.

The Job Interview

The interview is a two-way street. You're trying to find out about the candidate and decide whether or not he's going to be a good fit. He's doing the same to you. He's trying to decide if this is a company where he wants to work and if you're someone he wants as a coworker. Never assume people don't have choices, even in a recession. Also, in our connected world of social media, what happens in an interview gets around quickly. Treating a candidate badly may cut you off from a lot of people.

Up and to the Right

I periodically hear various claims that if someone looks up and to the right in an interview it means she's making something up, while up and to the left means that it's a real memory. Or maybe it's the other way around. And it might depend on whether she's right-handed or left-handed, or whether or not she's read an article telling her which way to look to appear believable.

Sometimes a glance is just a glance and an itch is just an itch. Don't try to read meaning into every little twitch or gesture. Most body language just isn't that subtle.

Listen to the Candidate's Story

A maxim in psychology is that the best predictor of the future is the past. What someone did in various situations in his past is a good predictor of what he'll do in a similar situation in the future. The more situations you look at, the more accurate your predictions.

For example, if you go out to dinner at a Chinese restaurant with someone once, you can't draw many conclusions from what he orders. However, if you have dinner with him many times, you may notice a pattern of dishes. That would let you predict with a fair degree of accuracy what he will order the next time you go out to dinner, or what to get him if you're bringing takeout back to the office.

By the same token, you want to get candidates to tell you their stories. You want to understand what they've accomplished and how they approach their jobs. Focus on actual events, not hypotheticals. Ask open-ended questions that will elicit detailed answers. Avoid yes/no questions when possible except to set up more open-ended questions. For example, do not ask . . .

> "What would you do if you were part of the team here and you didn't agree with the team's decision?"

Most people will give the answer they think you want to hear. Given a hypothetical situation, most of us generally assume that we'll behave in the most appropriate fashion. Instead, ask . . .

> "Have you ever been in a situation in which you disagreed with the rest of the team on something?"

Here, we're using a yes/no question to set the stage for follow-up. If they say, "No, that's never happened," you can ask them to describe how the team made decisions. Then ask, "What methods did the team use to come to agreement?" or "How did you avoid disagreements?"

Now we've got some open-ended questions that will start to tell us what role, if any, the candidate played in helping the team reach agreement.

If the candidate responds to the original question with "Yes," then you can ask for a description of the situation and then continue by asking, "How did you handle that disagreement?"

Again, we're exploring how the person behaved in a specific situation. We can then explore other similar situations and look for a pattern. It's also worth asking the candidate if her responses to the situations were typical or atypical in the environment. You don't want to ding someone for being argumentative if that's the norm in that company.

Whether someone tells you that she stuck to her guns and rammed her opinion down everyone's throats or she says that she solicited ideas from the rest of the team, sought clarification, and asked the other team members to explain why they disagreed, she is telling you something about how she solves problems. You have to decide which behavior you prefer, however, I will observe that someone who exhibits a history of not cooperating with teammates will probably not change just for you, and prima donnas rarely benefit a team.

It helps considerably to have multiple people interview the candidate and compare notes afterward. The candidate will probably describe the same situation differently to different people. Again, he's responding to the situation. None of us asks the same questions in quite the same way: differences in intonation, body language, surrounding conversation, time of day, etc., can trigger different details to pop up. You're looking for the broad patterns in a candidate's responses. The accuracy of any single statement is unimportant. What you want is his overall story.

After you've finished, don't evaluate the candidate immediately. Withhold judgment until the next day. It takes time to let the story percolate and for the patterns to emerge. It's also a good idea to give yourself a small break to allow any unconscious biases or automatic reactions to fade out.

Look at Different Situations

Most interviews are conducted in a fairly controlled environment: the office. This limits opportunities to see how the candidate deals with unexpected situations, interruptions, and other unknowns that will not arise during an interview in an office.

Look for opportunities to see the candidate away from office settings. In a recent article in the *New York Times*, Teresa Taylor, chief operating officer at Qwest, commented that she likes taking candidates out to dinner. This gives her a picture of how they handle a noisy environment, whether they drink too much, how they treat other people, and so forth. Sharing a meal with someone is also an excellent way to establish rapport. Showing you care about someone can be enough to make the difference between two or more competitive offers.

What About Interviewer Behavior?

As obvious as it may seem, make sure your interviewers are capable of interviewing. Many interviews are just an interrogation of candidates about their field of expertise because that's all the interviewer is comfortable with. To get the candidate talking, interviewers need to be flexible and adaptive. If they are rigid or view the world only in black and white, they're not going to be able to recognize good candidates who don't fit their image.

Interviewers who are unwilling to hire someone more knowledgeable than they are will doom the company to mediocrity. If your organization is highly competitive and employees are constantly being compared with one another, current employees are going to resist hiring anyone whom they perceive as serious competition.

Apparently there are interviewers who don't realize that they should give candidates their undivided attention. Would you hire a candidate who spent the interview reading e-mail or IMing? In one particularly egregious situation, the *interviewer* spent the entire interview reading e-mail. When the candidate complained, the interviewer's response was, "We multitask here."

That one statement spoke volumes about the organization's culture, none of it good.

If you do use tests, puzzles, or other problems, they must be presented by employees who are capable of understanding answers other than their own. It's not a battle of wits. The goal is to see if the candidate can solve the problem, not read the interviewer's mind.

Finally, you don't have any magical powers to tell if someone is lying or telling the truth. Hiring, or not, because you "just liked him" or "just didn't like her" is as often as not going to be the wrong decision. Gut decisions are great, but you first must train your gut! Otherwise, you may as well flip a coin. The candidate has probably had more experience in job interviews than you've had interviewing people.

HOW DO I CONVINCE THE CANDIDATE TO TAKE THE JOB?

It's common to put incentives on accepting quickly or time limits on offers. There's nothing wrong with that, especially if you phrase it as a necessity of the company planning ahead.

However, when you try to convince someone of something, she almost instinctively argues. Therefore, the best thing you can do is help the candidate convince herself.

The Art of the Offer

Before you present the offer, either as part of the interview or in a separate conversation, ask her what she thinks about the company. Specifically, ask questions like the following:

"Why do you think you'd like working here?"

"If we hired you and this turned out to be your dream job, what would have happened for that to be the case?"

"On a scale of one to ten, for which ten is 'absolutely,' how likely are you to accept an offer from us?"

When the candidate says seven, don't ask, "Why not an eight (or nine or ten)?" If you do, she'll tell you why she might not take the job. Instead, ask her, "Why not a five?" Let her tell you all the things she likes about the job. Then make the offer.

We'll go into negotiation in more depth when we discuss the gentle art of management jujitsu.

Don't Take Advantage

Far too many employers assume that when the economy is bad or someone seems desperate, the candidate will take the first offer you give him. Your offers should never leave a candidate feeling trapped or taken advantage of.

Once you've got him, you have to keep him. People won't stick around if they feel cheated or taken advantage of. They will leave the first chance they get, which will usually be at the point that is most inconvenient for you.

Also, you are not bargaining with your local butcher over a side of beef. You are trying to convince someone to focus his time and energy in a way that benefits you. You are trying to create a committed, motivated, excited employee. That's a long-term relationship, folks, and whether you start it on a bad note or a good one, you'll reap the rewards for a long time to come. Don't play games. Start people with competitive salaries and competitive benefits, and be generous with anything that is cheap for you but valuable to them. If you're asking people to take risks, recognize that and construct the offer appropriately.

For example, I frequently see start-ups being incredibly miserly with their stock. It's worthless! A fraction of a percentage here or there won't matter that much to you but can make a big difference to a candidate.

If you're asking someone to take a gamble on a company that hasn't been funded yet, be particularly generous on the stock front, and give them some sort of guarantee of salary when the money does come in. Respect the risks and sacrifices you are asking people to take on your behalf!

WHAT IF I HIRE THE WRONG PEOPLE?

Let's recognize something right now: no system is perfect. No matter how you select, interview, and test people, it won't always work. References can be helpful in some cases, but don't get overly invested in them. I've found that most people, when called, will find a way to give a good reference for the candidate, no matter how that person actually performed on the job. I learned this the hard way.

Frequently, the difference between being good and being an expert in a domain is not that the expert makes fewer mistakes; it's that the expert recognizes mistakes more quickly and moves more rapidly to cut his losses.

You will make mistakes. Sometimes you'll lose a wonderful candidate, and sometimes you'll hire the wrong person. In the former case, you can decide how much you want to chase after him. Sometimes it really is worth the effort, especially if you need someone with a very specific skill set that is in high demand. Frequently, though, once you've lost him, you won't get him to change his mind at that point. Leave the door open. Connect to him on LinkedIn or Facebook. Find an excuse to send him a card from time to time. Maybe that new job won't work out after all and he'll give you a call.

The other side of the equation is a bit more challenging. What happens when you hire the wrong person?

If we're talking malfeasance, ethical issues, dishonesty, harassment, and other such things, your legal department is the place to go for advice. It should already have corporate policies for dealing with such issues.

If we're talking about the employee who looked really good but just didn't work out, that's feedback. Learn from the experience. See if you can identify where your system went wrong and refine it. It won't always be possible. Sometimes the lack of fit could not have been predicted until the person was working in your environment. In a very real sense, errors are a cost of doing business.

Accept the mistake. Send them off with a generous severance package.

There are several good reasons for it: First, the mistake is at least as much yours as it is theirs. They've just provided you valuable feedback about your selection process. Reward them for their efforts. Second, the mismatch is probably not their fault. It's more likely to be something in the situation or your organizational culture. Third, as expensive as the mistake may be for you, it's much more expensive for them. Respect that. Finally, just because certain employees didn't work out doesn't mean that they don't know people.

By treating them with generosity and respect, you are creating a goodwill ambassador for your company. The dividends from that are immense: it can lead to referrals of highly qualified job candidates and product sales down the road. It can lead to someone who speaks well of your company to the press or on social media platforms. If things change, you might suddenly discover that former employee is just the person you need back.

A generous severance is a small price to pay.

Review Quiz

1. **Job analysis includes**
   a. Hard skills, soft skills, goals, and years of experience
   b. Hard skills, soft skills, behaviors, and goals
   c. Hard skills, goals, and willingness to work long hours
   d. Soft skills, behaviors, and years of experience
   e. Hard skills, goals, and good descriptions of tasks

2. **It is a true statement that**
   a. Looking up and to the right means someone is lying
   b. Candidates are always desperate in a recession
   c. Hiring is about understanding your objectives and finding someone who can bring those objectives to life
   d. Specific skills are always vital in all situations
   e. The interviewer can always trust his or her gut

3. **Subject matter experts for a job do not include**
   a. People doing the same job
   b. People doing a similar job
   c. Managers of people doing the job
   d. Coworkers who do a different job
   e. People who used to do that job

4. **Some typical job-related needs include**
   a. Safety, growth, variety, relevance, and autonomy
   b. Growth, variety, high salary, and autonomy
   c. Safety, variety, growth, and long vacations
   d. Variety, relevance, autonomy, and coffee
   e. A private office, safety, and autonomy

5. **When you hire someone, you are really offering him or her**
   a.   Money
   b.   A sense of power
   c.   Stock options
   d.   A vision of the future
   e.   None of the above

6. **Some ways of making an interview more effective include**
   a.   Listening to the candidate's story
   b.   Logic puzzles
   c.   Taking the candidate out to lunch or dinner
   d.   a, b, & c
   e.   a & c

5

THE MOTIVATION TRAP

O ne of the most common complaints that I hear from managers, CEOs, and company leaders is the phrase "They're so unmotivated!" or "Nothing I do motivates them!"

No one is ever completely unmotivated. What people are, however, is frequently motivated to do something other than what we'd like them to do.

WHY ARE THEY SO UNMOTIVATED?

I can't count the number of times I've heard about some "impossible to motivate" employee who is busily training for a marathon or something else that requires a tremendous amount of dedication, focus, energy, and, you guessed it, motivation.

What you're looking for are those employees who approach their jobs with the same level of dedication and focus that they approach training for a marathon or other activity. It's very hard to find those employees. It's easier to create them.

Motivation comes from many sources. It starts with the culture you've built, the vision you've created for your company, the goals you set, and your hiring process. Those elements make up your foundation.

Ultimately, motivation is a strong desire to do (or sometimes not do) something. That desire can be imposed from without, or it can come from within and be supported from without. You want the second.

Remember, no one becomes an Olympic athlete for the money, although some Olympians might end up making a great deal of money. Top athletes succeed because they are driven to perform at a high level. The money and the adulation only reinforce that drive. The ones who are out solely for the money are the ones who are most likely to give up.

PUSH, PULL, OR GET OUT OF THE WAY

In the Japanese martial art of jujitsu, the practitioner learns to not respond to a push with a push or a pull with a pull. Meeting force with force only creates opposition. While you might be strong enough to win some conflicts, eventually they take their toll. When someone pulls, you push. When someone pushes, you pull or you get out of the way. You don't oppose.

In jujitsu, the harder you make it for someone to stay on his feet, the harder it is for you to make him fall down. The goal is not to make it hard for your opponent to remain standing; the goal is to make it easy for him to fall down. The workplace is not all that different. Force creates opposition. Threats, fear, even many incentives, only lead to resistance. The very act of trying to force people to do something causes them to become suspicious and reduces their willingness to do it. It doesn't matter how much they might want to do it.

To be fair, I do hear from managers who insist that force works: they make sure their employees know who is boss and what will happen if they don't toe the line. There are problems with this approach. Constantly pushing people means that you can't see where you're going. All of your effort is going into the act of pushing. Sometimes they'll feel like you're going too fast. Sometimes they'll mistake an attempt to change course as a shove and resist, or they'll go too far and step to one side, leaving you to fall on your nose. The more you push, the harder it is to hit that moving target.

You want the employees who know where to go and why they should go there—and who understand how to get to their destination without you constantly having to force them to do it. You want a team so dedicated that if you don't get out of their way, they'll run you over.

Understanding motivation is the first step to getting such a team.

WHAT ARE THE PRECONDITIONS OF MOTIVATION?

"They have nice offices and top-of-the line computers. Why aren't they motivated?"
"We give them lunch every day! Why aren't they motivated?"
"They get a good salary! Why aren't they motivated?"

There always seems to be a litany of things that businesses do that just don't create motivated employees. The problem is that some things need to be in place before you can even start to think about motivation.

- **Comfortable working conditions are a must.** When people are cold, the lighting is bad, or the environment is noisy, it's hard to motivate them. Similarly, not having the tools you need to do your job makes people unmotivated. Having those tools does not produce motivation. Having the tools simply makes it possible to motivate people. Think goal-setting. If a goal is perceived to be impossible, then people won't try. You have to make the goal appear possible in order for people to become motivated.
- **Employees need to feel safe in the office before you can motivate them.** Feeling safe is not just about physical safety, although that may be an issue in some jobs. Emotional safety is even more critical. It is very hard to motivate people in an environment in which they fear mockery, humiliation, embarrassment, or loss of face. Despite how it may appear in the movies, fear is a remarkably poor motivating force. Fear makes people move away from the source of fear. Fear makes people fight back against the source of fear. What fear does not do is encourage people to work hard, innovate, or produce quality products.
- **Another part of that sense of safety is feeling that the job is stable and the pay is adequate to one's needs.** The more people are worried about making ends meet, about whether or not they'll have a job tomorrow, about their future, the harder they'll be to motivate. Again, resolving these issues does not produce motivation, but it does make it possible to motivate people.

WHAT IS THE MOTIVATION TRAP?

There is an apocryphal story that goes something like this:

> The famed psychologist William James Hall was once disturbed by a group of kids playing loudly below his bedroom window. Attempts to get them to play somewhere else failed. Eventually, the good doctor hit on a clever solution: he told the kids that the noise reminded him of his childhood and paid them each fifty cents to continue playing outside his window. The next week, he told them he couldn't afford fifty cents and dropped the payment to forty cents each. There was some grumbling, but, overall, the kids were happy to accept the money. This continued for about a month, with the payment dropping every few days. Eventually, Dr. Hall paid them a dime

each and told them that the next week they would get only a nickel. Infuriated, the kids stormed off, leaving him in peace.

Although the sums of money are very different, this same phenomenon is all too familiar to managers and CEOs. Businesses attempt to motivate employees with raises and bonuses. It works for a short time, but very quickly the reward or raise has to increase to produce the same level of motivation. When it doesn't, employees frequently lose motivation, and the best employees may leave the company for other opportunities. An alternate solution, not providing raises or bonuses, produces much the same results, only without the period of improved motivation.

The problem is that you have created a transactional, quid pro quo relationship. The bonus or the raise is presented as the goal: do this work well enough, get this prize. However, once someone attains a given goal, attaining the same goal a second time is inherently less interesting. Some managers decry this as laziness, when in fact, it is efficiency. Evolutionarily, the animal that uses less energy to attain a given number of calories has a selective advantage over one that uses more energy; it has more energy available for other tasks, such as running away from a predator who wants to eat it for dinner. Humans are remarkably efficient.

Furthermore, as challenges are overcome, people naturally seek greater challenge, with a corresponding expectation of greater reward. Consider an athlete who wins a small, local tournament. After a few wins, the local competition becomes boring. There is also an expectation that the reward for winning a more difficult competition will be greater than that for an easier competition. The same applies in business: with harder work, there is an expectation of greater reward. When the reward stays the same but effort increases, a feeling of diminishing returns is created that reduces motivation.

In a quid pro quo transaction, you are not looking at loyalty or long-term relationships. What you have is purely a fee for service arrangement. Motivation only lasts until the next reward or paycheck. Think about going to the doctor today, an experience that is all too often a quid pro quo arrangement. For those of you who had a family doctor when you were growing up, someone who recognized you and appeared to genuinely care about you, which was the more satisfying experience? Even when we hire consultants to help out our business, most of us want to work with someone who appears to care about more than the money.

In our example, Dr. Hall first tried to force the kids to go away. That failed. Eventually, he established a transactional relationship, in which they made noise in exchange for payment. By paying them in the first place, Dr. Hall shifted their goal from playing in a particular place to making money. Once he made money the motivating force, he had control over them. He could easily reduce motivation by reducing the money, until he eventually destroyed their motivation to play near him.

If you allow your goals to become all about obtaining short-term rewards and if you allow the relationship with your staff to become short-term transaction oriented, then you are falling into the motivation trap. When you view people's time as a commodity for which you pay them, you are falling into the motivation trap. You will be forced to spend ever more effort and create ever greater rewards in order to simply not fall behind.

That, as the old saying goes, is no way to run a railroad.

REWARDS AND FEEDBACK

Successful goal completion requires that you have clear, specific, measurable objectives and some means of determining that you're making progress. The ability of goals to motivate is dependent upon there being feedback during the process. Without feedback, it's impossible to tell how much progress you are making, and hence how far you have come. Looking back down the mountain to see how far up you've climbed is always more encouraging, more efficacy building, and therefore more motivating than looking up to see how much farther you have to go.

Checklists are one very powerful tool for maintaining a sense of progress. There is something visceral about being able to mark things off and see the list of accomplishments grow. How strong is this need to feel accomplishment? Oddly enough, saying to yourself that you are half done with something increases motivation far more than if you say to yourself that you only have half of it left to do. The two phrases may be mathematically equivalent, but they are not emotionally equivalent. Mr. Spock or one of his fellow Vulcans might not care, but the rest of us do.

Motivation is not always rational. Ignore the emotional side and you severely limit what you can accomplish. You'll also recall that the high-performance cycle uses the internal and external rewards resulting from goal accomplishment to build job satisfaction. Job satisfaction leads to increased commitment to the company, and hence an increasing willingness to accomplish the goals of the company. In other words, job satisfaction leads to goals becoming ever more relevant, which increases motivation to accomplish them and increases your personal sense of your ability to tackle ever harder goals.

Responding to Success

Therefore, your mission is to structure rewards as feedback on goal accomplishment, not as the goals themselves. Since most organizational goals are long term, lasting one, two, or more years, providing frequent feedback is even more essential.

Thus, when announcing a reward or even a raise, you need to place the event in context. Whether you do this in public or in private, highlight the accomplishment and remind everyone of the vision of the company. Connect the dots: explain how the accomplishment ties directly in to the company's vision and how the person being rewarded helped move the company toward its overall goals. The reward is a thank-you for advancing the company's goals. It is, quite explicitly, feedback that you are moving in the right direction.

Look for opportunities to celebrate progress. Again, a key point of maintaining goal motivation is recognizing success. You want to build the psychological momentum of victory.

Responding to Failure

Conversely, it's important to reframe failure. Failure has its own momentum, and it's not one that encourages people to work harder. Persistent failure discourages people and reduces motivation. Reframed, failure is just another form of feedback. When something doesn't work, you're being alerted to a potential problem. Failure gives you the opportunity to review your goals and figure out what's going on. When you develop the habit of viewing failure as feedback that lets you move forward with greater precision and confidence, you are less likely to be caught in a defeatist mindset and more likely to maintain the momentum of success.

Threats, warnings, and intimations of disaster that will take place "if people don't work harder" do not create motivation. They might create fear, and people might act out of fear. Eventually, though, people get tired of being afraid. The threat loses its power to evoke a reaction, although it does leave people feeling insecure. When people feel insecure, they are less likely to remain with your company and are easier for competitors to lure away. When the disaster doesn't strike, trust in management and the overall vision of the company are undermined. As children, we all heard the story of the boy who cried wolf and what happened to him. Don't be the CEO who cried wolf.

When Is It a Reward?

Why do companies reward employees? Perhaps the company wishes to recognize exemplary service; management wants to communicate that it's paying attention; the company is trying to highlight its values and expectations; or the company is trying to motivate other employees to step up and make that extra push. It comes as something of a surprise to watch one company take a slightly different approach.

The vice president of our old friend Shrinks-R-Us announced a new staff-appreciation policy to boost morale: each week, a staff member is recognized as the "Staff of the Week." Awardees are "invited" to write up a paragraph about themselves, which will be distributed to everyone at the company. Sounds good, right? There's a catch: staff members are not told why they were selected, and they are advised to leave out personal details from the paragraph since company e-mail might not be secure. As a bonus, you'll recall that SRU exports red tape, and employees generally do not appreciate being given extra paperwork.

The first winner "forgot" to include her name in the paragraph, and so it was distributed anonymously. In other words, an unknown person was given an award for unknown actions according to unknown criteria. There are a few minor problems.

First and foremost, it's not clear that the employees regard being chosen as a reward. In a classic "Star Trek" episode, Chief Engineer Scott finds it relaxing to spend his spare time in his cabin reading technical manuals. Going on shore leave is, for him, not a pleasant experience. When he's later confined to quarters, he's overjoyed. Granted, "Star Trek" was playing the scene for laughs, but it makes a very important point: a reward is only motivating if the recipient feels that he's been rewarded.

Next, the criteria for this award are shrouded in mystery. When it's a mystery, people are left wondering what behavior will get them the award and what will not. A tremendous amount of effort will be expended in trying to guess how to get, or how to avoid getting, the award. It's amazing what behaviors will emerge when people are trying to figure out the correct behavior to get a particular reward.

If you want to reward your employees, take the time to find out what they'd actually like. Make your award criteria clear and connect them to your corporate values. Demonstrate that you're actually thinking about your employees.

What Kinds of Rewards Work Best?

The first thing to recognize is that it's probably not what *you* want. You might view the latest Google Ultraphone as a wonderful toy that you can't wait to get your hands on. Your employees might not care. They might be satisfied with what they've got and not be interested in a new phone. You might view a week hiking in the frozen tundra of Alaska as a thrilling adventure and Hawaii as mindlessly boring. Your employees might love the idea of a week in Hawaii but find the idea of a week in the tundra less than wonderful.

If you really want rewards to motivate, find out what individual employees would like. While money is easy to give and rarely turned down, taking the time to find something appropriate for an employee is often not only less expensive for the company but far more motivating. The fact that you took the time to figure out what someone would really like magnifies the effects of the reward several-fold.

The nature of the reward also matters. Most rewards are *things*: money, gadgets, jackets, T-shirts, and so forth. The problem is that things are ephemeral. I've got a couple of fleece jackets that I still wear, but other than that, those bags, T-shirts, and gadgets are long gone. That first generation digital camera? Fun at the time, but hardly worth keeping. Something newer comes out, and suddenly your cool, new gadget is yesterday's old, boring gadget. Instead of increasing happiness, it causes discontent. Money is as like as not to go to paying bills.

Paradoxical as it may seem, while things are ephemeral, experiences are permanent. If you have an employee who loves snow hiking, that week in the frozen tundra may be perfect. The memory of an experience becomes part of who we are, and memories can last a lifetime. We do not grow as a result of things. We grow as a result of experiences. Figuring out what sorts of experiences a person might enjoy and then providing an opportunity to do that is one of the most powerful rewards available.

Let's unpack this and understand why experiences are so powerful. Things, as already pointed out, do not last. What remains are the memories associated with that thing, the fun it may have engendered. If it failed to produce much fun or if the memories don't stand out, the thing has no lasting power. No matter how different they appeared at the time I got them, in hindsight, one smartphone is much like another. My life didn't change in any noticeable way when I switched from a Treo to an iPhone. Experiences, though, shape us. They form strong memories that function as markers in our lives. Experiences are a chance to fulfill personal goals or spend time with friends or loved ones. The memories of an enjoyable experience don't become less enjoyable as we do other things or in comparison to what the people around us are doing.

Above all, experiences represent time, which is the one resource that we cannot save, invest, or get more of. We only get sixty minutes to the hour and twenty-four hours in each day. All we get to decide is how we will use the time, but, unlike money, it will pass whether or not we use it.

When you reward an employee with an experience, you are not just giving her memories, you are giving her time. The more personalized you can make the experience, the more powerful it is. You are not just giving a reward or providing feedback that she is helping the company succeed— you are demonstrating that you value her as a person. You are showing her that you care enough to invest your time on her behalf. Few things are more motivating.

The rewards you choose to give are investments in your employees, not expenses. That doesn't mean you should be irresponsible. It does mean that you get to choose the return on your investment. You can do the easy things that have a small return, or you can spend a little more time, effort, and, perhaps, money to provide the sorts of rewards that will motivate your employees not just today or tomorrow but next week, next month, and next year.

ROUTINE MATTERS!

One of the keys to successful motivation is to teach people to be optimistic. In other words, you must develop a success mindset. Optimism frequently gets a bad rap as foolish or naive. However, if you think about it, if you don't believe at some level that you can succeed, why are you starting? Motivation becomes easier when optimism is ingrained into the culture of the organization and into the routines that people develop. Unfortunately, many routines are created without deliberate intent and are as like as not to produce a failure mindset instead of an optimistic one.

Routines are habits that lead us through a sequence of events and produce a particular mindset at the end. For example, some people will always drink a cup of coffee and read the newspaper each morning. That puts them in the mental frame to begin the day. Successful athletes almost always have pre-competition routines that they practice religiously as part of their training. Like a habit, a routine becomes so ingrained that a person might not even realize that she is executing the same sequence of actions over and over. This is particularly true with an accidental routine. Unlike a habit, however, routines tend to fill the mind and thus guide the person from action to action.

The Routine-Mindset Connection

With repetition, the mindset that is experienced at the end of the routine comes to be the expected mindset; the person starts to anticipate it as he moves through his routine. Because the brain can only think about one thing at a time (despite claims to the contrary), the result mindset becomes the mental reality and eventually the expectation that fills the mind as the person contemplates beginning the activity. It's rather like the old joke from the classic Marx Brothers' movie, *Duck Soup*: Groucho is anticipating how a meeting with a foreign ambassador will go. He imagines holding out his hand and the other person shaking it. But then he wonders what would happen if the other guy didn't shake his hand. Within a minute, Groucho paints a dire scenario in which he rehearses how insulted he'd be and works himself into a state of righteous anger. When the ambassador finally shows up with his hand outstretched, Groucho slaps him across the face, yelling, "Refuse to shake my hand will you?"

In other words, the mindset you rehearse is the mindset you get.

Some people refuse to adopt any routines. This can be even worse. Without a routine, it becomes hard to focus on the tasks at hand. An effective routine helps someone concentrate on what is important—the paper to be written, the customer waiting for a reply, the software bug to be fixed, etc.—and ignore what is irrelevant, like the loud coworker in the next cubicle or the construction noises from next door.

When a large number of activities need to be fit into a day, a routine helps to organize the day and shape the time so that each activity leads into the next. Each block of time becomes a space in which a particular activity is the center of attention. Even in business settings where the day is full of unpredictable events, short routines can help restore focus and concentration after an interruption.

A Caveat on Routines

Some routines are small, involving individuals. Some routines involve the entire office, department, or organization. Sometimes even the best routines can become stale, devolving into meaningless ritual. When people are going through the motions without any sense of intention or caring about the results, you know that your routines are no longer working.

When that happens, it's time to shake things up. Do something different and fun. Change the scenery. Get people out of the office for a day or two. Juggle responsibilities for a day or treat people to a movie. Change the routines to be more dynamic.

Although we're programmed to like a predictable environment, too much predictability can turn into boredom. When the routines start getting stale, people are in danger of becoming bored or burning out. Fortunately, the very staleness of the routine is your canary in the coal mine. Make use of it.

IT'S A MARATHON!

As the old saying goes, "Success is a marathon, not a sprint!" Once upon a time there was a software company developing an innovative data management tool. When it started, everyone was excited about the product and eager to be part of such a novel project. Three years later, the software was on the market. Naturally, everyone was ecstatic and eager to buckle down and produce the next version.

Well, not exactly. Yes, the product was on the market; after that, the tale has an unhappy ending. Over time, all that energy and motivation steadily eroded, as a result of poor planning, long hours, overly optimistic deadlines, interpersonal conflict, a bad habit of "motivating" by moving from crisis to crisis, and other stressors.

Motivation is not something you do once and then forget about. It's an ongoing process. When you stop motivating employees, the marathon is over, whether or not you've reached the finish line.

Vision Quest

Review the material on vision in Chapter 3. Create a vibrant vision of the future: remind people why they became excited in the first place. Refresh and revise that vision as the project evolves. Help your employees see their place in the vision. Help them build their own personal vision, tied to the company's vision. Encourage employees to imagine success; daydreaming is a powerful way for people to stay in touch with their, and the company's, long-term goals.

Managers need to act as coaches and cheerleaders, helping employees maintain focus and remain upbeat even when things are going poorly. For those who like to draw a distinction between management and leadership, managers must become leaders. Managers must help the employee build confidence, establish routines, and set realistic, difficult goals. They need to remind employees of past successes, not past failures. The latter only decreases motivation and confidence. If managers do not already have the necessary skills, the business needs to see to it that they acquire them. Managers who are glorified individual contributors will not be able to fill this role, and the entire team will suffer as a result. Every top sports team has a coach, no matter how good they are.

Get Out of the House

Look outside the company. Encourage employees to join professional associations and network with their peers. Online social networks are a start, but face-to-face interaction is better. Make it possible for employees to meet with customers and hear from them how they will benefit from the company's product or service. It's easy to become discouraged when working for a faceless "other." It's easier to become excited when the person you are helping has a face.

Encourage employees to attend industry trade shows and conferences. Sure, it may take them out of the office for a few days, but it helps them keep tabs on their field and expand their knowledge. It also helps keep the office routine from becoming stale.

Growth Opportunities

Never stop learning. Providing training for employees both increases their skills and increases their loyalty and motivation. Don't restrict training to classes that are obviously job-related. You never know what's going to turn out to be useful. Encourage people to explore and learn new material whether or not it appears useful.

Relationships Have Power

For anyone, putting a picture of a spouse, kids, family, or close friend on his or her desk is another powerful motivator for many people. It's easier to make an effort when we are reminded of the reasons we're making that effort. No matter how much you may "know" you're working to help your family, the visible reminder still helps.

Contain the Annoying Stuff

Avoid letting unpleasant tasks fill the day. Whether you are a CEO, manager, or individual contributor, no matter how enjoyable the job, some of the work is not much fun. If the unpleasant parts fill the day, motivation swiftly declines. Unhappy people are motivated to get away from the source of unhappiness, not work harder. Therefore, allocate a chunk of time each day to performing unpleasant tasks.

When you promise yourself you'll work on something for "an hour," you're more likely to continue well past that than if you leave the time open-ended. Setting the goal of working on something unpleasant for an hour means that at the end of that time you will have a sense of completion and satisfaction. Encourage and help your employees to construct their schedules with this concept in mind.

An added benefit is that the sense of completion happens even if you decide to keep going. Now you're feeling virtuous because you are doing extra work on an unpleasant goal. If you leave the time open-ended, you never feel that sense of completion and satisfaction for getting an unpleasant job done. Instead, you've created a sense of failure. It is success that gets people coming back to do more.

Move Forward by Walking Away

Paradoxically, you can increase both productivity and motivation by encouraging employees to take breaks. Although this may sound counterintuitive, stepping away from your work is one of the most powerful means of making progress. An hour break to go to the gym can yield greater progress in solving a problem than eight hours spent banging one's head against the wall. People who take vacations experience significantly less burnout than those who do not. The eureka moment rarely comes when we're exhausted and frustrated. It comes when we do something else, something to shake ourselves out of the mini-rut we've gotten into.

Finally, encourage your employees to take hobbies and family obligations seriously. Strange as this may sound, people who are devoted to something outside the office are more productive, not less. Knowing that practice or dinner with the family is at 7 P.M. means that there is greater motivation to finish work on time. The more success on the job enables people to experience their lives, the more motivated they'll be.

Leaving in time, whether or not the work is finished, actually increases motivation to do more the next day. It's when there is nothing else on the schedule that work expands to overflow the time available. Also, by recognizing that employees have a life outside the office, you are actually building the relationship between them and the company. When you respect someone's boundaries and build a strong relationship, that person is more likely to make that extra effort on your behalf when it's needed. I used to chase my direct reports out of the office if I found them working late "just because." If there wasn't enough to do, they should just go home. We all knew there'd be times when another department would be running behind schedule and that time would be short when the ball finally got passed. As a result, when the periodic crunches hit, I never had to ask them to work late or come in on weekends. They did what needed to be done.

DON'T BE CHEAP

I've spoken a great deal about how and when to use monetary rewards and how making monetary rewards the goal is extremely destructive to long-term motivation. However, there is one guaranteed way to make sure that people will become totally focused on rewards and on extracting every penny possible from the company: act cheap. When the organization looks like it is cutting corners on the backs of the employees, you undermine motivation and create suspicion.

Rewards don't need to be lavish. Rewards, and policies, do need to appear fair.

One professional organization was looking for ways to cut costs. They had traditionally provided dinner to members of one of their committees in exchange for asking them to come to evening meetings. They considered holding the meetings but no longer paying for dinner. After consideration, though, they decided to handle things by continuing to cover dinner, but not drinks or dessert. They also took the time to explain to members why they were cutting back. Not only did no one mind paying for their own dessert, the action subtly reminded people to pay attention to what they were ordering for dinner and consider less expensive dishes.

WHAT ABOUT VOLUNTEER ORGANIZATIONS?

I frequently get asked about volunteer organizations. After all, they can't pay huge salaries, so how do they keep their volunteers motivated? The huge salary by itself is only a small part of the issue. In a volunteer organization, the vision and the sense of purpose are absolutely critical. It's important for the organization to not take the volunteers for granted or treat them as interchangeable, just as it's important for a business to not treat its paid employees as interchangeable.

The argument is often made that there's a big difference between a volunteer and a paid employee. While there are certainly differences, there's also a great deal of similarity. In fact, considering what we've discussed thus far, one can argue that virtually everyone is a volunteer—it's just a question of whether they're paid in cash, benefits/perks, recognition, or some combination.

Fundamentally, the organization is making a deal: in exchange for a certain level of value provided to the organization by the volunteer, the organization will provide some form of recompense or recognition for that effort that demonstrates that the volunteer is contributing to the success of the organization. Recognition is doubly important. The organization is showing that it appreciates the volunteer's efforts, and the volunteer is receiving solid evidence that the work he is doing matters to the organization. No one likes to spend his time doing something that doesn't matter.

When the organization reneges on its end of the deal, it risks alienating the volunteer. Worse, it's telling the volunteer that it doesn't actually care about her contribution—that it's clearly not all that valuable to the organization or the organization wouldn't be so cavalier about it.

Not a great way to maintain motivated volunteers.

So what should the organization do? Optimally, it should honor its commitments. However, if there are real economic reasons why it can't, then the organization should be preemptively open about it.

In other words, as soon as the organization knows that it can't meet its obligations, it should notify everyone affected. Lay out the situation: not "due to the bad economy," but "due to an unexpected drop in enrollment costing the organization x dollars and unexpected expenses in the areas of this, that, and the other thing," and so forth. The more specific and open the organization is, the more forgiving people will be. In fact, they are likely to work even harder on behalf of the organization; after all, if they're volunteering, it's probably because they care. The people running the organization should lead the way by reducing whatever perks or benefits they get.

When things are bad, the instinct is to circle the wagons and not communicate. All that does is alienate those who would help. Instead, demonstrate trust by bringing people in and being open with them. Not only will it keep the volunteers motivated, but you might just get some unexpected, novel ideas that will benefit the organization.

MOTIVATION AND FLOW

Remember our discussion of flow? Because a flow state is so enjoyable, it is also one of the most powerful motivators available.

When you have clear goals and the opportunity for people to focus without interruption, you can get that flow state to occur. It can happen to individuals or to a team.

One of the biggest advantages of a predictable office environment is that it's easier for people to lose themselves in their work. When people are being constantly forced to shift from one task to another, concentration, focus, energy, and overall enjoyment suffers.

The more you can create an environment in which your employees can lose themselves in their work, the happier and more productive they'll be, and that will translate to your bottom line.

Why wouldn't you want that?

Review Quiz

1. **Which statement is true?**
   a. Motivation must be imposed from without.
   b. Motivation is caused solely by large salaries.
   c. Threats are an effective form of motivation.
   d. The best motivation comes from within and is supported from without.
   e. Prizes are great motivators.

2. **Having the tools you need to do your job is**
   a. A good idea, but dedicated people will make it work anyway
   b. All that's needed to motivate someone
   c. An expense to be managed
   d. A necessary precondition of motivation
   e. None of the above

3. **The motivation trap is**
   a. Pushing your employees instead of getting them to pull
   b. Paying more and more just to maintain performance
   c. Making the reward or paycheck the goal
   d. b & c
   e. a, b, & c

4. **The best rewards are usually**
   a. A really nice T-shirt
   b. The latest hot gadget
   c. Tickets to the opera
   d. Money
   e. The opportunity for the recipient to do something she has always wanted to do

5. **A good motivational technique is**
   a. Making the day unpredictable in order to keep people on their toes
   b. Constant interruptions
   c. Reasonably consistent routines
   d. Rigid rules that govern every minute of the day
   e. None of the above

6. **Which of the following are good ways of increasing motivation?**
   a. An exciting vision of the future
   b. Managers who act as coaches and cheerleaders
   c. Contact with customers
   d. Taking breaks
   e. All of the above

CHAPTER 6

POST-HEROIC TEAMS

A flashlight is a wonderful tool. In a dark room, it's exactly what you want to help you avoid finding furniture unexpectedly. A laser is also a wonderful tool: it can drill a hole in a piece of steel, remove a cataract, serve as a pointer during a presentation, or make a wonderful cat toy. While a laser may not be very useful for finding your way in the dark, the range of things a laser can do is quite remarkable. Even more remarkable is that, like a flashlight, a laser is nothing but light. The difference is in the focus. Diffuse, you have a flashlight; concentrated, a laser. A laser is powerful and versatile because, metaphorically speaking, each ray of light is helping and supporting the others. In a flashlight, each ray of light is independently going in the same direction.

What a team is capable of accomplishing is also determined by its focus. An unfocused team, which we'll call a "horde," is slightly less useful than a flashlight. If you send them into a room ahead of you, you can count on them to find the furniture in the dark . . . just listen for the crashes. At least the flashlight doesn't damage the furniture. They can certainly get work done, but it takes an immense amount of effort to keep them motivated, on track, and cognizant of the company's goals. In a horde, each member is concerned only with his or her own success. The goal is to be the hero. If everyone succeeds, then the horde succeeds. If some fall by the wayside, well, the heroes did their part and will reap the rewards. To the would-be heroes, it matters less how well the larger organization or company does than how well the individual performers do.

A team, on the other hand, is considerably more useful. A team is focused. Team members see success as something jointly, not individually, achieved. Each team member knows that success comes from working together, sharing knowledge and resources in pursuit of a common goal. Indeed, a highly focused, highly effective team will utilize all resources available with a minimum of waste. The members act on the knowledge that the task is too big for any one person to carry alone. Effective teams are post-heroic. In other words, they help and support one another and are dedicated to accomplishing the goals of the company rather than being out solely for themselves.

THE MISSING "I"

When I speak on team building, it is around this point that someone in the room exhibits an apparently uncontrollable need to remind everyone present that "there is no 'I' in 'team.'"

While there may not be an "I" in "team," a team is made up of individuals. There are three "I"s in "individual." What does a team do? Well, we hope the team will win. There's an "I" right there in the middle of "win." Oddly enough, you can't win if you take out the "I."

It's critical for a team to be able to work together and for members of the team not to be competing with one another. It's equally important that each member of the team feel that he or she is an integral part of the team's success. Without that personal connection, it's extremely difficult to get people excited about the work. If you don't feel like you have a personal stake in the outcome, if the vision doesn't speak to you and the goals do not feel relevant, you will not be committed to the company or the outcome. Commitment is an individual experience.

Unfortunately, I frequently see companies treating team members as interchangeable parts, not as unique individuals. Not only does this undermine the team, it is also a tremendous waste of resources. A major advantage of having a team is that you have access to multiple eyes, ears, hands, and brains. Each person brings unique skills, knowledge, and perspective to the problems the team is facing. When a company fails to take advantage of those people, then it is spending a great deal of money for very little return.

In the Mann Gulch disaster, Wagner Dodge failed to appreciate the perspectives and opinions his team brought to the table. He relied solely on his own eyes, ears, and brains. Had he bothered to obtain information from the rest of his team, it is highly likely that most of them would not have perished under Dodge's command. When the team has no "I," the team cannot see.

On the flip side, some companies go too far in the other direction. One company spends so much time on "I" that there's no time left for "we." It has no team; there's only a group of people who happen to be wandering in vaguely the same direction. Meetings are characterized by constant jockeying for position and arguments over turf. Different groups in the company see themselves as competing with one another for the favor of the CEO. Oddly enough, the level of excitement and commitment in this situation is about the same as the one in which there is no "I." When you have too much "I," no one can agree on what he or she is seeing. Too much "I" or a missing "I" produces much the same degree of blindness.

When you have a team that is all "I" and no "we," then you also have people who are afraid to bring in anyone who might be viewed as competition. When the converse is true, the same thing happens. Only the people who are willing to blindly submerge themselves in the team are viewed as good team players. The people who are the best at getting things done are going to be far too threatening to the status quo to be allowed in the door.

WHY TEAMS FAIL

Some twenty years ago, I had a rather odd experience while working for a Silicon Valley software company. As we came closer and closer to shipping the product, more and more problems would crop up: not problems with the software, as one might expect, but interpersonal problems. There was an increase in arguments, bad feelings, and ineffective conflicts at exactly the point at which it would seem most likely and logical that people would be feeling the greatest sense of unity and triumph. I experienced the same phenomenon at other companies. In more than one instance, the team successfully snatched defeat from the very jaws of victory.

The teams at each of these companies I just mentioned had never truly learned to work together, to handle disagreement, or to tolerate variations in working style. The only thing the software team had ever agreed upon was the necessity of getting the product out by a deadline. The strength of that agreement forged sufficient common ground for the team to work together. Unfortunately, as the project drew nearer and nearer to completion, the glue holding the team together became weaker and weaker. Would everyone start fighting again? Would people leave the company? Working with people you don't always agree with is easier than working with complete strangers. The old cliché is often true: better the devil you know than the devil you don't. Ironically, people would engage in the very behaviors they were most afraid of in order to delay the completion of the project and keep the team intact.

The great benefit of teams is that they provide a variety of skills and perspectives. The great weakness of teams is that they provide a variety of skills and perspectives. In order to reap the benefits of having a team, the members of the team need to share a common vision, recognize what is important, and know what should be tolerated or ignored. Effective team building involves more than just agreeing on a set of goals, especially since agreement on goals is difficult to get when team members cannot even agree on how to work together. It involves building a common language, a common set of values and beliefs about how to work, how to interact, and how to behave. In other words, the team needs to create its own culture within the larger culture of the organization.

The early days of the team's existence are extremely important. How many professional sports teams go into competition with a team that's just been assembled? Very few. Of those few, how many win? Even fewer. Basketball fans might well remember the Olympic Dream Team of a few years ago, made up of some of the best basketball players in the United States all playing on the same team. While they were certainly competent, they did not demonstrate the level of brilliance everyone expected. Despite their individual excellence, they never really came together as a team.

The only difference between business and sports when it comes to team performance is the belief in business that a team can be assembled and instantly jump to performing at a high level. It simply does not work, no matter how much we may want it to. A team in this situation is particularly vulnerable to cracking under stress at exactly the moment when team members most need to be working together.

WHAT IS THE LIFE CYCLE OF A TEAM?

It takes a great deal of effort for people to learn to work together effectively. If that effort isn't put in up front, then it becomes an ongoing demand on employees' concentration and attention. A sports team that isn't prepared will crack under the stress of competition; people will make careless errors, become distracted at critical moments, and start arguing or pointing fingers. In business, the same thing occurs; the frequency of mistakes goes up, communication between employees decreases, people find it harder to concentrate on work, and there is a greater incidence of argument, one-upmanship, and jockeying for position.

Teams need to create common ground. The more similar the members of the team are, the easier this process is; however, homogeneity comes at the cost of lower overall performance. Teams that are initially more heterogeneous are harder to forge into a cohesive whole but generally make for stronger teams. Greater heterogeneity leads to more varied approaches to problem solving. Similarly, a very structured, hierarchical communication and power structure makes for early positive performance, but performance degrades rapidly as the problems become more complex. A more open, democratic, nonhierarchical system yields much better performance on complex problems but takes longer to start producing results.

The most important lesson around dealing with teams is recognizing that teams go through a distinct and unavoidable life cycle, and this cycle takes time. Some managers tell me that there is no time for such nonsense! Their teams will perform immediately. These are usually the same people who are complaining months or years later that their teams are not performing, that the same problems and arguments keep cropping up, that they have high turnover, and so forth.

The life cycle of a team is best described by Tuckman's stages of team development, named for Bruce Tuckman, a psychologist who first developed the model in 1965. These stages are Forming, Storming, Norming, Performing, and Adjourning. Susan Wheelan, another psychologist whose work has focused extensively on group dynamics, further details and extends Tuckman's model. Her work has been verified in businesses, nonprofits, school groups, and so on, in around fifty different countries.

People on the team behave differently in the different stages of team development.

Teams progress through the first four stages in order. It takes five to six months to get to the Performing stage, assuming that everything goes perfectly. This rarely happens. In fact, fewer than a quarter of all teams ever reach Performing, and more than half never get past Storming. Since Storming is also quite possibly the most unpleasant part of team development, getting stuck there is not a recipe for happy, productive, motivated employees.

Note that work gets done at all stages. The only question is how much effort and energy you have to put in. Teams in the Forming stage use up a lot of energy for little return, while teams in the Performing stage get hugely outsized returns on their efforts.

There is one exception to teams moving through the stages in order: going backward. While you can't unbake a cake, you can unbake a team. Sudden shocks, too much turnover, too rapid growth, overwork, and burnout can all cause a team to regress. A team may drop back a single stage, or it may drop all the way from Performing to Forming in a blink. Should that happen, it must climb back up again.

Forming

In many ways, this is the most critical stage. Forming is characterized by a great deal of uncertainty and discomfort. People tend to be overly polite and tentative. The biggest fear is of being excluded, of the group suddenly realizing that you don't actually belong or you realizing that you're in the wrong place. In a very real sense, the members of the team have not yet really committed to being there. Your high-performance cycle is not yet running; team members have not yet internalized the goals of the company. Problems are rarely discussed directly, which can cause misunderstandings to balloon into major divisive issues.

During this phase, team members determine whether or not they feel emotionally and intellectually safe working with one another. They develop a sense of group identity or remain a collection of individuals. In some teams, this manifests by work being put off until the looming deadline forces people to come together. In other teams, one person takes over and tries to do all the work herself. Fundamentally, team members have not agreed on how they should work. They don't understand each other's working style or approach to getting things done.

There's an old saying that a couple isn't really married until they've had their first fight. The same is true of teams. Part of working together involves arguing with coworkers—put any group of people together, and they are bound to have their own approaches and solutions to problems. If team members feel unable or unwilling to argue with one another, they avoid conflict. If they are forced to argue but haven't developed effective means for conflict management, the argument can quickly turn personal. In either case, the exchange of thoughts and ideas is blocked, anger builds, tension mounts, and the ability of team members to work together is severely compromised. Instead of developing group identity, team members may become convinced that their best strategy is maximizing personal gain instead of team performance.

The most important thing you can do during Forming is increase members' sense of comfort and belongingness to the team, essentially building their sense of safety and community. At the same time, you should take care to not go so fast that you lose the use of your "I." Team members need to become comfortable discussing not just what the work is but how they will do it. They need to recognize that different people have different approaches and develop comfort and trust in working together. There is a strong tendency in this stage for members to rally around you, the leader, and for dissent and discussion to be quashed. The idea that there is no "I" is particularly prevalent at this point. It's simple and attractive and makes people feel good in the short term, but going that route will lead you down a blind alley. Whenever someone says there's no "I" in "team," remind him about that "I" right in the middle of "win."

During Forming, members will typically not ask many questions. Everyone assumes they understand what the goals of the team are, and no one wants to look bad by admitting otherwise. When managers ask if anyone has questions, the usual response is silence.

In Forming, team members often take on roles or parts of the project for reasons that have little to do with their actual expertise or interest. They might do it out of a sense of obligation or for fear of exclusion if they don't. Frequently, they do it because they don't clearly understand the goals. In one case, the VP of a certain company assigned critical roles based on the clothing that people were wearing. The person whose shirt reminded him of the database expert in his last company was assigned the database piece of the project. . . .

The most important thing you can do is help your team develop good discussion and problem-solving skills. This requires a great deal of patience and directive leadership. Your team has little sense of its own skills and abilities at this point and is likely to bite off more than it can chew. Remember that goals that are too large can easily become overwhelming. Guide your team to early, small successes in order to help them develop an awareness of their strengths and weaknesses and to develop confidence in their abilities as a team.

It is quite common for a Forming team to divide work up according to arbitrary measures of fairness as opposed to practical measures of getting the job done or value of results. Thus, members will frequently insist that everyone spend the same amount of time working or always be present at the same times. Members who work quickly are told to spend more time on their projects, whether they need to or not, and are viewed as "getting ahead of themselves." Members who work slowly may be seen as lazy or not committed. In fact, since both the roles and the tasks are fairly randomly assigned at this point, both perceptions are illusory and need to be redirected early, before they become divisive.

A mark of Forming is that work never gets done when the leader is not there. This is only because no one actually understands the goals and the team doesn't yet have the confidence, knowledge, or skills to make effective decisions in your absence. It would be a mistake to respond punitively, though. Work not getting done is not the problem; it's a symptom.

You, as the leader, have the most, possibly the only, well-defined role in the group. That gives you a tremendous amount of power and probably an almost irresistible urge to use it. Resist. Like a judo master, learn to use your strength as little as possible and only when absolutely necessary. Coercion never leads to high performance.

Eventually, if you do your job well, the members of the team will start to care. This can be a moment of great joy or great pain, depending on your response. The process takes at least two months. Trying to force people through it faster seems to fail approximately a hundred times out of a hundred. The odds are not in your favor.

Storming

Frequently, I see teams have one or two small disagreements, perhaps about the time or place for a meeting, how to set the agenda, or what to order for lunch, and assume that they've now survived Storming.

There are times when you get the flu and it feels like getting hit by a truck. There are other times, though, when you feel bad for a day or two and then it seems to go away. Then, about the time you think, "Whew, that wasn't so bad!" you get hit by the metaphorical truck.

The Storming stage is like that. It frequently comes when least expected, after you have started to feel comfortable and safe. Just at the point when you feel like you know what's going on with your group and their behavior has started to become predictable, pow!

The very sense of safety and personal investment in the goals of the team that you need in order to achieve productivity also sets the stage for Storming to begin. Because your employees now feel comfortable on the team, because they now feel like they belong, and above all, because they now care, they start pushing back. They have their own ideas about how things should be done. Whereas during Forming they would accept your opinion with little or no discussion, now someone is as likely as not to say, "Well, I think that's a really stupid idea!" When I'm speaking on or teaching leadership and team formation, I always ask people how they'd respond to that person. Whether my audience is college students, managers, or executives, the most common answer is, "I'd show him!"

This is also the wrong answer. It cripples initiative, risk-taking, and innovation. It can either paralyze your group or lead to more conflict later. When you engage in the conflict, whether you win or lose, you still lose.

Remember that personal goals will trump group goals. As your employees start to care more and more about the project, the disparity between their personal goals and the goals of the group becomes stronger.

In Storming, everyone has an opinion. Everyone knows the "right" way to get things done, and it's usually the way that works best for them. Everyone wants you, the leader, to stand up and provide direction. Of course, if you actually do this, practically everyone then complains that you're being a dictator. What they really want is for you to tell everyone else to shut up and do things their way.

Don't be surprised if half your team thinks you walk on water and the other half would like to see you facedown in the water.

In Storming, team members are openly discussing and arguing how the team should work, who should be doing what, what responsibilities and accountability mechanisms need to exist, and so forth. Far too often, decisions are made simply to stop the bickering rather than to actually resolve the issues. Create space and impose breaks in the discussion if things get heated.

Remember that role assignments made during Forming are somewhat random. This is the time when people will start becoming more obviously unhappy in their roles. Allow and encourage experimentation. There will be some inevitable mistakes, but that's the only way you're going to be sure you have the right people in the right roles at the right times.

It is particularly important at this stage that mistakes be treated as an opportunity to evaluate and adjust, not judge and punish. You are setting the ground rules for how your team deals with disagreement and error. Punishment at this point leads to people either withholding information later if they think that information could hurt them or tattling if they think they can gain status or reward through hurting someone else. You are shaping your culture actively at this point.

Heroic behavior will often become manifest in Storming, although it can sometimes start during Forming. Heroic behavior is when people put in dramatically long hours or otherwise make sure that everyone notices their extreme sacrifices on the part of the company. I've seen this behavior in a number of environments, particularly technology companies, when someone spends all night fixing bugs at the last minute. The only minor flaw in the whole thing is that in almost every case the employee had written the buggy software in the first place. The engineers who had written clean code and had finished debugging before it was a crisis were often viewed as less dedicated. Heroic behavior looks impressive but is frequently an illusion. A characteristic of later stages of team development is that members pitch in to help one another without fanfare, and people who avoid the problem in the first place are recognized.

Pay careful attention to whom you speak. Do you find yourself communicating with only a subset of the team and relying on them to spread the word to the others? Sending e-mails to everyone on the team or holding meetings at which you address the entire team doesn't count. The informal paths of communication matter even more. You must actively work to keep communications open with everyone on the team. That may mean seeking people out, inviting them to lunch, or finding some common interest.

You also need to be aware of the general flow of communications in your group. Does everyone feel comfortable talking to everyone else? The answer, unfortunately, is usually no. Find ways to break down barriers to communication without using force or imposing draconian rules. Manage focused discussion, keep debates and conflicts about the issues, not the people, and remind people of the vision of the company and why you're all there.

If you're successful, you will create the foundation for a very strong team. You will enable your team to engage in potentially heated debate without losing sight of the objectives. You'll also create a team whose members understand how to best work with one another and are tolerant of one another's work styles. No one should feel that he or she is always the one giving in.

In short, you are creating an atmosphere of trust, which is no easy task. More than half the teams in the business world fail to get past this point. Never forget, the increased productivity is more than worth the effort to make it happen. Storming typically lasts at least two months, and once again, the odds of speeding it up successfully are about the same as for rushing through Forming.

Norming

Norming is characterized by the development of trust and the formation of organizational structure. There is a developing balance between "I" and "we." Teams at this point have learned to argue effectively. Members are communicating with one another in a fairly open structure. If they aren't, odds are you either haven't reached this stage or it will collapse under stress and revert to Storming.

As your group enters Norming, you will see a greater ability to focus on group tasks and goals. There won't necessarily be less argument, but the argument will be productive. Members are actually starting to act like a team. They are more open to giving and receiving feedback, asking questions, and raising concerns with the processes and outcomes. In terms of goal-setting, you'll see greater understanding of and commitment to the organization's goals. Team members not only care about the vision, but they are starting to believe that they can make it happen and that their efforts matter to the group. The team also has a much clearer idea of its own capabilities. They have a better understanding of their strengths and weaknesses and the best ways of approaching problems. This developing skill in problem solving needs to be nurtured for the team to continue to improve.

As the team gains more confidence, you'll see a greater degree of trust. This will translate into a greater willingness to form subgroups to handle particular tasks. In earlier stages, there's a strong tendency for the entire team to take on everything, or to view the work as something to be done by a collection of individuals. Now you are starting to see a more sensible and effective division of labor and status on the team. You'll also start seeing members spontaneously helping and encouraging one another.

As the group matures, the leader often finds that he must give up many of the trappings of power. In one of those paradoxical moments, the more power you give up, the more power you have. We'll discuss this further in the next chapter. For now, recognize that many of the tasks of the leader become tasks of the team, such as supporting one another, interfacing with the outside world, and organizing meetings.

The biggest danger in Norming is that it can become a period of enchantment. Particularly if Storming was extremely intense, members of the team may be so relieved at finally reaching some sort of modus vivendi that they are unwilling to rock the boat. Good as it feels, the development of the team is not yet complete.

Norming typically lasts a month or longer and is, again, difficult or impossible to speed up. Approximately 25 percent of teams get stuck here.

Performing

If you've reached the Performing, or high-performance, stage, congratulations! You have a post-heroic team! Just getting here is an accomplishment. Now that you've arrived, the hard part is maintaining that level of performance. As Susan Wheelan, among others, notes, the degree of performance of a team at this stage is greater even than at Norming. Surgical teams that have reached Performing have significantly higher success rates than those that have not. Emergency room teams save more lives. Product development teams produce higher quality products with less failure work. Sales teams sell more. The list goes on and on.

If you have a small task that needs doing, you are better off giving it to an existing post-heroic team than creating a new team to deal with the task. The post-heroic, high-performance team will dispatch it almost casually. A high-performance team is characterized by a laser-like level of goal clarity. They understand the vision, they know their roles in it, and they have clear-cut goals oriented around bringing that vision to life.

The team now understands how to utilize all available resources. It will spontaneously and automatically adjust itself to bring the strongest combination of people and skills to bear on any particular problem. Team members know their jobs and how to help other people. That doesn't mean that everyone is an expert in everything; that's neither possible nor realistic. Rather, members know how to give and receive help. As a result, the team is more effective, knowledgeable, and productive than any individual or group of individuals.

The most difficult part of leading a high-performance team is keeping it at that level. To someone not involved and not knowledgeable about leadership and team dynamics, it can look as though you, as the leader, are spending most of your time doing nothing. Like an airplane pilot, you are, in fact, spending long periods apparently doing nothing. However, during that time you must be constantly alert and aware of the signs of trouble lest you miss your airport and fly for an extra two hours. One of the biggest obstacles to a team achieving, and maintaining, high performance is a manager who doesn't understand how to lead it.

The biggest danger a high-performance team faces is burnout. Maintaining high performance for long periods is physically and mentally exhausting for team members. If they push too hard for too long, they'll destroy themselves. Just like the coach of a top-notch athletic team, your job is to remind them to take breaks, rest, recharge their batteries, and keep their focus. Many leaders find this extremely difficult; they are so locked into the mindset that people need to be pushed that they don't know what to do when they need to apply the brakes instead. The greater the intensity of the work, the more important it is to take breaks.

The higher the performance of your team, the more the concept of the eight-hour day or the forty-hour week is an illusion. The team will do what it needs to do. If they can do the job in less than the sacred eight by forty, great! Don't worry about the time; worry about the results. Your job is to pay attention to when their concentration starts to slip and to keep them from pushing through the fatigue. Remember, the role of the governor on an engine is to prevent the machine from running so hot that it destroys itself. If your team starts to burn out, you could easily find yourself back at square one.

Another big problem faced by high-performance teams is boredom. The duties of the team or the project the team is working on can start feeling like the same old, same old. Most serious athletes periodically have to break up their routines, change their training, and do something different and new in order to maintain focus and interest. A high-performance team is no different. The process needs to be kept interesting, or performance will decline and the team will regress. Your job is to monitor the team, paying attention to how they're feeling and acting. Find ways to change up the daily routine; invite suggestions for fun activities or for ways to make the day different. Remember, this is a high-performance team. They're good at solving problems.

Adjourning

There are some groups that continue on forever, even as members come and go. The U.S. Congress is such a group. For those who listen to the speeches, the concept of forever can take on a whole new meaning. Athletic teams are another example: the Boston Red Sox have been in continuous existence for more than a hundred years, even though the players keep changing.

Most organizational groups have a definite life span. Sometimes the dissolution of the group is planned, sometimes it is unplanned. Groups might be assembled to handle a specific project and then disbanded afterward, or a group may be terminated by the closure of the company or the early termination of the project.

As discussed earlier, when the group is held together primarily by the goal of completing the project, approaching that goal can lead to increasing group dysfunction.

In general, the dissolution of a team is often stressful and unpleasant for its members. People may engage in a flurry of work in an effort to deny the inevitable. Argument may increase and communications begin to break down. When the ending is abrupt, such as a company going out of business, there is sometimes a tendency to blame others on the team.

It is not unusual for members of the team to look for ways of continuing together past the official termination of the team. For example, I worked many years ago at the IBM Palo Alto Scientific Center (PASC). Even now, almost twenty years after PASC closed, some members still meet for lunch. There is still a member directory and occasional announcements of major accomplishments from members or their children.

It is very important for the leader of a terminating team to be aware of the stress that the event is causing in the lives of the team members. Remind people of their accomplishments and what they did to bring about the team's vision. Build people up at every opportunity.

HOW DO I BUILD MY TEAM?

Team development takes time. You can't change that. Management and employees must both be aware of and comfortable with the idea that building trust does not happen instantly. It's not easy to develop that intuitive understanding of other people's work style. Despite their popularity, most team-building exercises are counterproductive at worst, useless at best.

Mistakes are not personal, and they're not a sign of failure. They're inevitable. An environment that does not allow mistakes does not allow learning.

Managers need to act as coaches: focus on successes and help employees appreciate the skills each person brings to the table. Just as a coach with an athletic team, managers need to be more directive with younger teams or newer members of established teams. In each case, the goal is to enable the members of the team to function more and more on their own, with the manager eventually acting mostly as advisor, strategist, sounding board, and chief encouragement officer.

There is often tension between building affiliation with the team and the company and providing each person with as much freedom to work the way he or she wants to work, or autonomy, as possible. Don't let autonomy destroy affiliation or affiliation destroy autonomy. You need both to be successful.

Creating or providing something that is visibly shared helps create common ground. Creating common ground between the members of the team helps them get to know one another and feel comfortable with one another. You are building team identity. It can help to come up with several ways to reinforce team identity, giving people a choice in how they define themselves. Allowing people autonomy implicitly recognizes their competence and your trust in them. Denying autonomy questions competence and undermines trust.

Build a series of small successes. Each success helps the team develop confidence and an increasing sense of its own abilities. Keep the pace of work relaxed at first, and then increase it as people become increasingly comfortable with one another. If you've done things right, you'll soon find yourself running to keep up, and you'll find your team far more productive than if you'd tried rushing forward right out of the gate. Just like in sports, if you don't warm up, you can end up flat on your back.

Competition within the team is not a sign of progress. It is, however, natural in the early stages of team development. Competition needs to be refocused outward, so that the team is competing against a deadline or against other businesses, but not against one another. As soon as you create internal competition, you are creating a team of heroes. When a team member insists on competing against the team, it can be very helpful to demonstrate to that person that the team as a whole can outcompete him. If that's not true, if you really do have one person on the team who can outcompete the entire rest of your team, then either your goals are not well defined, or you need stronger team members.

Review Quiz

1. **A team of heroes is**
   a. Highly focused
   b. Efficient
   c. Dedicated to the goals of the company
   d. Motivated to help one another
   e. None of the above

2. **Which of the following are the stages of team development in order?**
   a. Forming, Norming, Storming, Performing
   b. Forming, Fighting, Whining, Complaining
   c. Forming, Storming, Norming, Performing
   d. Forming, Storming, Resting, Adjourning
   e. Forming, Running, Practicing, Working

3. **Forming is characterized by**
   a. Vitriolic argument
   b. Laser-like goal clarity
   c. Tentative, sometimes overly polite conversation
   d. Mutual helping
   e. Lack of leadership

4. **Which of the following is true about team development?**
   a. A ropes course is an excellent tool for building strong teams.
   b. Team development takes time.
   c. A strong team is all "we" and no "I."
   d. Leaders must rule with an iron fist.
   e. A strong team can run full speed out of the gate.

5. **The advantage of a team is that**
   a. It provides the leader with a group of flunkies
   b. Henchmen are good for getting things done
   c. A team provides additional hands, eyes, ears, and brains
   d. It provides a reason to have managers
   e. It is always the best way to work

7

THE ROLE OF EMOTIONS IN LEADERSHIP

I was once asked on a radio show what a leader looks like. My answer was, "Whatever we think a leader looks like."

From the moment of empty radio silence, I inferred that this was not what the host expected me to say.

WHAT IS LEADERSHIP?

We view leaders in the context of our cultural biases and beliefs. We view as a leader someone who fits the cultural image of a leader. For example, at one company, the founder was slender and clean-shaven. For years after his death, there was a tendency to only promote people who were slender and clean-shaven. Unfortunately, the fact that someone looks like a leader doesn't mean that person will be a *good* leader. Leaders will behave according to their cultural beliefs about how a leader should behave, even when that is not the best way to lead in the specific situation they are in.

Fundamentally, leadership is the art of getting people to do what you want because it's what they want. It is the art of enabling people to see that they will benefit by following you and then keeping them excited and enthusiastic about doing it. Using force to get people to follow you is not leadership—it is coercion.

That said, there are times when a leader needs to provide some very directive leadership. This is particularly true with the early-stage teams discussed in the previous chapter and when adding new members to existing teams. *Directive* does not equate to coercive. As we learn quickly in jujitsu, coercion only generates resistance. *Directive* means providing people with the structure they need to move forward and become productive. It means making it possible for team members to experiment and explore, to become contributing members of the team and take the team past where you imagined it could go.

One of the most frequent questions I get from students and professionals alike is, "What is the difference between leadership and management?"

Leadership and management are not identical, nor is one better than the other. They are complementary skills. To a great extent, the job of a manager is to keep employees moving safely along well-traveled paths, to build their strengths, and to help them excel in their roles. The job of a leader is to take them off into uncharted territory and bring them back safely. Most effective leaders spend a certain amount of time managing, and many managers can lead if they are willing to take some risks.

At the end of the day, if you can't bring yourself to take risks, you'll never be an effective leader.

"NEVER TELL ANYONE TO DO WHAT YOU CAN'T DO . . ."

I am always fascinated when a manager tells me that she would never ask her employees to do something that she couldn't do. A team that limits itself to the abilities of the leader is not really a team. It's a group of henchmen who may be good at carrying out instructions but who are not capable of achieving high levels of creativity or performance. It would be like Captain Kirk refusing to order Scotty to fix the warp drive on the *Enterprise* because Kirk can't do it himself.

In an effective team, the abilities of the team are greater than the sum of the individuals. It is the capacity of the team to work as a unit and to be able to put the right person or subset of people in the right place to deal with problems that makes the team strong. I once worked with a software company that had the idea that every engineer should become expert in every other person's code. Unfortunately, this was a fairly large project, and the different pieces required different areas of highly specialized knowledge. Each of the engineers had spent many years building up that expertise and could not simply transfer it to every other engineer. While having partners working together makes a great deal of sense, trying to have everyone doing everything is self-defeating. It sacrifices the benefits that come from applying specialized knowledge to specific problems.

WE'RE ALL LEADERS!

Periodically, I hear from students and professionals alike that "we're all leaders here." While this may be a nice sentiment, the reality is that it doesn't quite work.

The image of the leader as the person who tells everyone what to do, approves all decisions, and controls all aspects of the group has just enough truth in it to be dangerous. As you'll recall, when a group is first assembled, there is a high degree of uncertainty about the goals of the group and how the members all fit in such that they are quite happy to have a certain amount of very directive leadership.

Fundamentally, however, a group cannot have multiple people setting the agenda, calling the meeting times, establishing goals, and performing certain other administrative functions. Someone has to be in the position of providing the structure and managing the group's dynamics. If not, what you have is apathy and chaos: the more disorganized the environment, the less people are inclined to make an effort.

Teams always have a leader, whether or not that person is officially recognized in that role. I always assign students in my psychology and management classes to group projects. I am continually fascinated by the number of students who tell me that their group succeeded without any leader and then proceed to describe how one member of the group took charge and led the project. Sometimes, the person telling me there was no leader was, in fact, the leader and didn't even realize it.

A team without a leader is a disorganized horde. Conversely, a leader without a team is just some joker taking a walk. The two are intimately tied together. A great leader in one environment and for one team might be a terrible leader in another situation: Steve Jobs is a fantastic CEO for Apple; Colin Powell was an amazing general. Now, imagine Steve Jobs running the military or Colin Powell as CEO of Apple. On second thought, maybe that's a scenario better left unimagined!

We are not all leaders. However, we are all members.

In the end, the leader is just another team member. Many leader behaviors are also member behaviors: everyone is responsible for helping to build the team, supporting the developing structure, fleshing out the vision, and so forth.

POWER AND LEADERSHIP

Power is a funny thing. Many people want it, but when they get it, they discover that it's not nearly as useful as they expected. Having the power to tell someone what to do sounds wonderful, but it's hard to compel someone when you need them as much as they need you. Pushing critical people too hard runs the risk that they'll exert their power to leave. Power can also be extremely deceptive. It's important to understand what power is and how it manifests, after which we can discuss how to effectively apply power.

In an organization, we are typically looking at five bases of power. Three of these are based in the organization or surrounding culture, and two are based more heavily in the individual.

· **Legitimate power** is the power that is bestowed upon you by the organization through the various means by which that organization awards power. Becoming a manager in a company is one way of gaining legitimate power. In the United States, winning an election bestows upon the winner significant power, for example, the role of president of the country.
· **Reward power** is the power to grant rewards to your followers. Those rewards are often tied directly to the organization. Raises, bonuses, extra vacation time, and more interesting projects are all rewards that draw from the manager's legitimate power. Reward power generally implies legitimate power; however, the converse is not necessarily true. As a manager at one company, I had legitimate power, but all rewards had to be approved by the CEO. As a college professor, I have the power to award grades based on work. The meaningfulness of my reward power is a direct result of my legitimate power that derives from my position.
· **Coercive power** is the power to force others to do our bidding. It is the power to punish. A manager may not be able to grant someone a raise, but she may be able to dock someone's pay. Coercive power also derives from the organization and usually involves some form of sanction, the ultimate of which is exile, better known as being fired. It's worth mentioning that exile from the group is a very powerful threat, and hence should be used sparingly. Excessive use of coercive power is not good leadership; it's thuggery.
· **Expert power** is the power that accrues to someone through that person's specialized knowledge or expertise. The more necessary and unusual

or difficult that knowledge or expertise is to obtain, the more potential power it can bring. Being an expert software engineer can bestow a huge amount of power in a company in which those skills are badly needed. Expert power can be transformed into legitimate power through the granting of titles or other symbols of authority. For example, the black belt both confers legitimate power and proclaims the wearer's expert power. The titles Senior Engineer and Chief Engineer both make statements about the bearer's level of knowledge and may also confer legitimate power.

- **Referent power** is the power that you gain through the respect and admiration of others. This power can never be granted but must be earned. It can be earned through the use of any of the other forms of power, however, the overuse of reward and coercive power can easily destroy your referent power.

Being hated and feared does not create referent power. Conversely, being loved as the provider of all good things does not create true referent power either. Buying people's loyalty only puts you into the motivation trap. When your reward power runs out, so does their loyalty. True referent power comes from being an inspiration, a role model, and an example—someone whom others admire and wish to emulate. It comes from being someone whom others feel they can trust and can count on. It comes from connecting yourself and others to something bigger than any of you. Properly used, referent power is the most effective form of power. People will do what you want because what you want becomes what they want.

Shifting Power from the Coercive to the Influential

These bases of power can be viewed as cultural, forceful, and influential. Legitimate power and, to a lesser extent, reward and coercive power can also be viewed as external power, or power that is given to you that can be taken away again. Expert and referent powers can be viewed as internal powers, or powers that are part of who you are. While it is possible to imagine scenarios in which reward and coercive powers are internal, those are unlikely to come up in a business environment.

Legitimate Power

Legitimate power derives its effectiveness from the forces of culture and tradition. We live in a culture that acknowledges that certain people in certain positions of power have the right give us instructions. Businesses inherit that concept. The manager is assumed to have the right to give instructions to employees. Second line managers have the right to give instructions to first line managers, and so forth. Violation or support of those cultural assumptions typically trigger the organization's mechanism for reinforcing the cultural beliefs: in other words, the activation of coercive or reward power by the person in charge. If these cultural assumptions are not supported through the use of other power bases, if the rules can be broken with impunity, those rules will cease to have value. In turn, those people who derive legitimate power from those rules will lose their power. Eventually, certain people or certain job titles will no longer carry legitimate power.

Reward Power

Reward power derives its effectiveness from your ability to provide people with valued rewards. It doesn't involve convincing people that they should want what you want, nor does it assume that people actually care about anything other than the reward. Reward power also requires the resources to provide rewards.

Coercive Power

Coercive power requires that you have both the capability and the willingness to punish people who are not doing what you want. As simple as coercive power may appear, it's actually anything but. In most companies, about the only unambiguous punishment you can apply is firing someone, with all the hassle that entails. It's also not a very effective threat in that you aren't likely to use it unless you really, really mean it. It also doesn't change the person's behavior if you do carry it out. That can be a consideration if your goal is to produce a change in the person's behavior. What about other sanctions? An extremely difficult thing for people to recognize in an organization is what constitutes a reward and what constitutes a punishment: many more subtle sanctions are not noticed or are misinterpreted. At one company, the CTO would assign people certain tasks that were supposed to indicate his displeasure. Unfortunately, while they were presumably tasks that he didn't like to do, they were not necessarily tasks that the people to whom they were assigned found unpleasant. In fact, some of them thought they were being rewarded!

Another problem with coercive power is that coercion doesn't decrease resistance, it actually increases it! While you will often get a short-term change in behavior, the offending behavior will often become stronger if the person believes that she can no longer be coerced or if she decides she doesn't care.

You'll notice that, like reward power, coercive power does not involve convincing people to do what you want because it's now what they want. It just involves forcing people to do things in order to avoid punishment. Galley slaves will work hard to avoid being whipped, and they'll abandon you the first chance they get.

It is quite possible that you are getting the impression that there is never any appropriate use of coercive power. That's not the case at all. I am, however, saying that it must be used sparingly, judiciously, and fairly. If employees do not perceive its use as fair, it will do more harm than good. It is fully appropriate to use coercive power to discipline an employee who is violating the rules or norms of the company or acting inappropriately toward others. In some cases, it may be appropriate to apply coercive power when someone is not meeting performance goals, although it is very important to understand the specifics in such situations. We'll cover that in more depth when we cover giving feedback. One secret to using coercive power well is to pay attention to the situations in which you feel you need to use it: can you identify points at which an earlier intervention would have allowed the use of less coercive power or avoided it entirely?

Also, while reward and coercive powers can be used easily in the first stage of team development, their use will frequently come back to haunt you in the second and third. If overused, they may prevent you from getting past Storming. Too much pent-up resentment can prevent the team from progressing or even cause it to regress.

The final two bases of power, expert and referent powers, do not come from the organization and are not directly coercive forms of power. They can be used coercively to some degree; however, they are generally less effective when used in such a manner.

Expert Power

Expert power works through your knowledge and understanding of a domain and your ability to function at a high level in that domain. An engineer's knowledge forms the foundation of her expert power. Expert power serves primarily to advise and suggest courses of action and predict likely outcomes based on expert knowledge. Expertise draws its power from the trust people have in the expert's ability to apply her power in a way that helps the organization. An expert who is not trusted or not believed has no power.

Many managers complain that they cannot be expected to be experts on the technical subjects that their direct reports are working on. Other companies insist that every manager must be a technical expert. Both are misunderstanding expert power. The goal of the manager is not to develop expert power through being a top engineer but to develop expert power as a manager. Managers need to develop management expertise. Similarly, if you develop your leadership skills, then you will gain expert power as a leader. Being an expert leader is the first step to gaining the respect and hence the trust of your followers.

Referent Power

This is the ultimate in influence power. Referent power works because people like, respect, and trust you. Referent power is, in a very real sense, your reputation. If you have high referent power, you need little in the way of legitimate power to be effective. If you lack referent power, you will find that your legitimate, reward, and coercive powers are like performing surgery with a club. You can build referent power by acting in a manner that others will admire, by setting a good example, and by not shirking from the difficult decisions. As a leader, it's important to visibly live up to the ideals that you espouse. By doing so, you build your referent power. The more you act to enable others, the more you build up your referent power.

The leader who develops his expert and referent powers eventually reaches that point at which he has the power to not use power. Doing this effectively, though, requires understanding the role of certain key emotions.

UNDERSTANDING KEY EMOTIONS IN LEADERSHIP

I hear all the time about how there is no room for emotions in the office. Yet, the companies where I've seen this implemented are only putting on a front. Under pressure they are as emotional as anyone else. I still remember, from early in my consulting career, the manager of a team screaming at me that he did not allow emotions to influence his behavior. For some odd reason, the irony of the moment was lost on him.

I am frequently asked how I can tell whether or not emotions will really matter to a team. Is there some reliable way of recognizing when you have a prospective employee who will not be influenced by such unpredictable, unprofessional, and messy things as emotions? In fact there is. Computers and robots are not emotional. In the event that you have robots interviewing for jobs at your company, you can be reasonably sure that they will not act based on emotion.

If you're dealing with people, that means you're dealing with emotions. You can't deny it, avoid it, or prevent it. Therefore, it helps to understand which emotions really matter. There are four that form the basis of most organizational behavior: fear, affiliation, autonomy, and competence. The secret to being an effective leader is understanding and being able to manage these four emotions well.

Fear

Fear is an amazingly popular motivator, in large part because it is so easy to use. Just because it's easy to use doesn't mean it's useful, though.

Fans of Mel Brooks's 2,000-year-old man might recall that he described the primary means of motivation in "those days" as fear: when the lion popped up, you were motivated to run the other way. Fear is very effective at getting people to move away from something. Scare someone enough and he'll move very rapidly away from the source of that fear even if that means slamming full tilt into a tree.

Despite its popularity, fear leaves something to be desired as a way of motivating employees. In one of my first jobs out of college, I got "the talk." It was my first or second day on the job at a Silicon Valley start-up, and the VP of engineering stood over me and lectured me about how high his standards were, what was expected from employees at a start-up, what would happen if we didn't measure up, and so forth. At the very end, he said, "And I'm a serious hunter. I have several guns at home. What do you do for fun?"

The effects of his talk were easy to see in the behavior of the team: blaming and finger-pointing were the norm, not cooperation and problem solving. This was less a team than a horde, bravely charging forward in vaguely the same direction, each member quite willing to hang another out to dry.

Fear, however, does not manifest just as a "motivational" tool. Fear has a way of influencing a great many decisions. Hiring can drag on for weeks or months because everyone involved in the decision is afraid of hiring the wrong person. Actually, let's be more precise: people are usually afraid of *being blamed* for hiring the wrong person. Fear of blame undermines creativity, innovation, and problem solving. If people are afraid of punishment for being wrong, they will not take risks or initiative. When people are scared, they do not work for the good of the team or the company; rather, they work for their own good.

When a leader is scared, that fear can infect and demoralize the team. That guy who liked to hunt? He was afraid that the start-up wouldn't work, and he attempted to manage his fear by scaring others into acting in ways that would reduce his fear. This is a big reason why fear is so pervasive and often so subtle—if we're not gibbering with terror, we may not even realize that we're afraid. We just know that we feel uneasy and so we take actions to reduce that discomfort. If those actions succeed in the short term, we tend to engage in them more because of the relief they bring us. The problem is that we may not be succeeding at what we think we're succeeding at.

Actions that appear to work become habits and eventually part of the culture, which can create a culture in which employees are always feeling tired and burned out, reducing productivity. People look for some sense of safety in a job. Feeling scared, or working in a culture based around fear, reduces that sense of safety, making it difficult to recruit or keep top people.

"Houston, We Have a Problem . . ."

Part of leadership is projecting confidence. One of the prerequisites for a successful team is that the team must believe that it will be successful. When the leader looks scared, the team will be scared and will eventually lose confidence in itself. It is the leader's job to calmly identify the challenges ahead and project the necessary air of confidence to his team. In the movie *Apollo 13*, Gene Kranz doesn't ask what's not working in the *Apollo* capsule; he asks what *is* working. By so doing, he stops the deluge of bad news and focuses everyone on the resources they have to work with.

In a very real sense, the opposite of fear is not courage but optimism. Courage is the ability to go ahead when you are scared. Optimism is the belief that you can and will succeed. Fear, ultimately, is the belief that you will fail and that failure will lead to terrible things happening. The future you focus on is the one you'll end up with.

Affiliation

The first emotion to encourage is affiliation or relatedness. You might also think of it as team spirit or a sense of community. When people come together to form a team, the first thing they do is look for common ground. How they find it makes all the difference. In the absence of a leader actively building affiliation, the team will unite around anything. This might involve uniting against a member of the team who keeps a different schedule or who dresses differently; it might mean going to lunch at a particular time. Uniting around the leader is fine to a point, and necessary in Forming. However, if the affiliation is not transferred to the vision and goals of the company, the team may never make it out of Forming.

To really create affiliation, the leader needs to actively get to know team members and encourage them to get to know one another. Take the time to find out what people like and do not like, what their hobbies are, what they do. This will also help you with motivation and in designing appropriate incentives and rewards for members of your team.

The leader who shows appreciation for the outside-of-work accomplishments of his team members will motivate them to accomplish more at work. By encouraging team members to get to know and appreciate one another, the leader creates a team whose members support one another and are not afraid to admit mistakes. Creating strong bonds of affiliation makes it easier for team members to give and accept help from one another. A good leader will also convey a vivid image of the goals of the team and rally the team members around that image.

Autonomy

It is possible to take the concept of affiliation too far. When you start believing that you have no "I" in "team," then you are going too far. The strength of the individual is the team, and the strength of the team is the individual.

How important is autonomy? At one company I worked with, the new CEO's vision involved very substantial changes to the way training was conducted. Existing trainers went ballistic. They saw the new policy as undermining their authority, compromising the mission of the company, and reducing the quality of their classes. In short, they saw threats to their autonomy. The board was having doubts that they had hired the right person. It wasn't long before all parties were so busy screaming at each other that none could hear what the others were saying. It was at about this point that the chairman of the board called me. My solution was to help both parties develop stronger affiliation. Once the employees got to know the CEO better, they began to trust that she wasn't trying to tell them how to do their jobs;

as she got to know them as individuals, she realized why her initial actions, well-meaning though they were, had provoked such a strong reaction. They are now doing quite well.

Fundamentally, autonomy is more than just letting people work the way they want to work. Autonomy is trusting people to get the job done without your needing to watch them or direct them all the time. You can't do that if you're afraid to trust your team and if the goals are not sufficiently clear.

Trust comes through building affiliation and developing the power to not use power. Think about it this way: if you believe that your team only works because they fear you or the coercive power you can exercise, or if you believe that they are only working because of the rewards you can offer, then you'll never fully trust them to work when you're not there. That means, in turn, you'll never be comfortable giving them autonomy.

If you want your team to achieve maximum effectiveness, you need to let go. Just like the parent who is teaching his child to ride a bicycle, at some point you have to let them go with the full and certain knowledge that your team will fall down or run straight into the neighbor's mailbox.

The key is to build autonomy slowly. Team development is neither instantaneous nor is it heralded by trumpets and large signs. It is a gradual process of development. You build autonomy by giving your team easy tasks to accomplish at first, tasks that are within its appropriate level of team development. Create a series of small wins or small successes. Each small win creates momentum and helps build your confidence and trust and their confidence and trust.

The other key point is that autonomy is a consequence of structure, not lack of structure. Part of what enables you to trust a team with autonomy is your knowledge of where the team is, what it is doing, and how it is doing it. That means having sufficient structure in place that the team members can easily keep you informed without feeling that you're looking over their shoulders. Too much structure is stifling; too little is chaotic. Structure comes from having clear and well-defined goals.

If the goals of the team are unclear, then the team will be unable to work without you providing direction: the team will be stuck in Forming or Storming. If the goals are clear, then the team can work freely, and you can tell where they are by paying attention to which subgoals are being accomplished. In other words, feedback is as important to you as the leader as it is to the team. You need it so that you can judge how well things are working and continue to provide the appropriate balance of autonomy and direction; they need feedback in order to know whether or not they are being successful and how well they are progressing toward the company's overall vision.

Competence

Finally, the last critical piece is competence. I'm not talking about hiring competent people, but about creating an atmosphere of competence.

Fundamentally, you can focus on one of two things: you can focus on failures, and make dire predictions about what will happen if someone screws up, or you can focus on successes, and remind employees of the things they did well. The former is going back to fear. The best way to encourage someone to work harder, to tackle more difficult challenges, to put in that extra effort on behalf of the company, is to build her up, not tear her down. People are energized by memories of success.

When you remind people of successes, you are also recalling specific experiences to mind. Remember that experience is an extremely powerful motivator: when you remind people of previous obstacles that they overcame or other problems that they solved, you are re-invoking in them that optimistic mindset and can-do attitude that is necessary for success.

Remember that the team has little sense of how good it is, especially early in the process of team development. Individuals also tend to be highly inaccurate at judging their own competence in a new situation. Therefore, they instinctively look for an external gauge to tell them how competent they are. The leader is that gauge. The more you demonstrate your confidence in them and the more you build their sense of competence, the more competent they will become.

Nothing succeeds quite like the expectation of success.

WHAT ARE AVOIDANCE BEHAVIORS?

As the name implies, avoidance behaviors are actions people take to avoid working, to avoid loss of face or feelings of incompetence, or to avoid dealing with the rest of the team.

The two most common avoidance behaviors are "I can do it myself," and social loafing. Not working when the leader isn't present we've already discussed as characteristic of early-stage groups.

"I Can Do It Myself"

Often there is a tendency of one person to try to take control of the group, doing all the work or at least attempting to dictate to everyone else the "right" way to do their jobs.

Justifications might include these:

- This task is not appropriate for a group, or we can't figure out how to divide it.
- The group is too big. There are more people on the group than are appropriate to the task.
- I feel that I'm in competition with everyone else in the group, and this is the way I can win. (This is especially common when compensation is based solely on individual performance and/or when there is a strong culture of blame and finger-pointing.)
- Doing it myself makes me feel safe and builds my competence and autonomy.
- I have nothing in common with the group. (This is normal in early-stage groups.)
- I don't trust/like/respect the rest of the group, or they don't trust/like/respect me. (This is also common in early-stage groups.)

Social Loafing

By contrast, social loafing is the tendency of one or more group members to not contribute to the group and let the others carry them along. Social loafing is often associated with the following attitudes or conditions:

- The group is too big for the task, and I feel unnecessary or as if my contribution is valueless.
- The task is unitary. It should really be done by one person, and if I'm not that person, there's nothing for me to do.
- I don't buy into the goals. They are not personally relevant to me, and I don't really care if they are achieved or not. I don't see how I will benefit.
- I'm in competition with others, and I want to see them "lose." (In the Storming stage, this is especially likely if it's seen as a chance to knock someone else down a peg or gain status in the eyes of the boss.)

- I'll reap the benefits anyway, so why bother?
- I'm more anxious about being in a group than about the consequences of not doing the project.
- I'm preserving my autonomy.
- I'm afraid that I can't do it, and I don't want to risk my feelings of competence.
- I believe I have nothing in common with the group.

Symptoms of a Different Problem

It's important to view behaviors such as "I can do it myself" and social loafing as symptoms, not as problems. The actual problem is usually one of the possibilities given in the bulleted lists. Only by understanding which problem or problems are manifest is it possible to develop effective solutions. Dealing with anxiety or lack of affiliation is very different from dealing with someone who is determined to compete with the rest of the group at any cost.

However, it is also possible that the person who is competing is doing so out of anxiety or to avoid admitting a perceived lack of competence.

Thus, a single incident often does not provide enough information to correctly evaluate the situation. Instead, when diagnosing group problems, we have to practice becoming aware of what we do not know and then asking questions that will help us get that information.

Symptoms enable us to find the problem, but the symptoms are not the problem. We'll come back to this later.

STRATEGIES FOR BUILDING TEAMS

Let's start by returning to the emotions of autonomy, affiliation, and competence. Key to helping people navigate team development is to help them learn how to build on these emotions and become aware of how their own behavior is influencing these emotions in others. Remember, not everyone is a leader, but everyone is a member. The more members who adopt these "leader" behaviors, the more effective the team will become.

These strategies take practice! Role-playing scenarios are a great way to give team members that practice. Skills that are not practiced are significantly more likely to fail under stress.

Much as I hate to say this, we also must recognize that sometimes the team just doesn't work. Not all teams are successful, whether in for-profit or nonprofit entities, whether in sports or in business. Sometimes there isn't a good skill mix, cultural or personality clashes are too strong, group members dislike each other too strongly, or a preexisting history cannot be overcome, etc. The more skilled you and your team members become at these strategies, however, the better your odds of success.

•   **Start by strengthening affiliation.** Members need to look for ways to build connection with the other people in the group. Remember, a Forming group is looking for identity and something to rally around. The more that people can find those connections, the easier it is to keep the group focused.

•   **Part of building relatedness can also involve admiring the accomplishments of other people on the team.** Find something to praise: Maybe one of the other members is a serious athlete or has kids who are good at sports. Show genuine admiration for her skill. At the same time, share activities and accomplishments that you are proud of. Don't compare. One isn't better than another. What you're doing is building their status and your status at the same time; admiration is always more valuable coming from a peer. Not only are you building relatedness, you're also increasing their (and your!) sense of competence.

You can also build competence by soliciting ideas, taking notes, and showing that you're listening. Express appreciation for their thoughts. Save the critical examination for later, after you've all generated ideas on how the team can work best. Praise successes, whether group-related or not. Make it a goal to find something to praise about a different coworker each day.

•   **Ask for input, increasing autonomy and competence.** "What concerns do you have about this solution?" "How can we improve this?"

As the group starts to define its goals better, invite people to suggest a timetable. Give people flexibility in deadlines as much as the project will allow.

Establishing deadlines and checkpoints gives people clearer goals, increased feelings of competence, and improves their sense of autonomy because they're not being bugged.

•   **Avoid resorting to threats.** Threats increase fear, decrease affiliation, threaten autonomy, and produce resistance. It's better to say something along these lines: "If we can't figure out how to work together, what's going to happen?" or "How do you think we can better work together on this?" Give people the opportunity to build autonomy and competence by recognizing the seriousness of the situation on their own.

- **Look for ways to save face for everyone.** Embarrassing people does not produce cooperation. Instead, it attacks competence and damages affiliation.
- **Work from the beginning to develop a participative form of decision making in the group.** This can be difficult because many early-stage groups will be unwilling to make decisions and leave it to the leader. Then they'll complain later. When they do make decisions, many groups have a tendency to vote too soon. Find out if people are ready to decide.
- **Conflict is inevitable. How you handle it is not.** Practice reframing conflict: instead of meeting aggression with anger, reverse it. "You're wrong!" can be met with "That's possible. What problems do you see?" instead of trying to prove you're right.

    Mildly self-deprecating humor can be an extremely effective way to defuse tension. Another response is, "Hey, I'm making this up as I go along, and I'm running out of ideas. I could really use your help."

- **Focus on process.** Decompose outcome goals into learning goals and process goals. In other words, instead of being focused only on the results, help your team understand what behaviors will generate those results. This increases competence and allows for greater autonomy because each person can better understand what each of the others is doing.
- **Recognize that each person may have skills that are not obvious at the start.** Equivalent work does not mean identical work. Help develop fair divisions of labor that capitalize on each person's strengths.
- **Encourage team members to talk with everyone on the team.** Be polite, be friendly, keep communications open. At best, you'll help the group develop an open and flexible communications structure, which helps the group in the long run.
- **Emphasize that asking one another for help is not a bad thing!** Teamwork is an activity of mutual helping. If members feel that asking for help will come back to haunt them when reviews come around, or if they feel that asking for help means that they will be viewed as less competent, then your team will never make the best possible use of the strengths and expertise of its members.

Finally, lead by example:

- If you want to be listened to, first listen to others.
- If you want to be praised, praise others.

- If you want to be respected, respect others.
- If you want to create mutual helping, be willing to seek and accept help.

WHAT IF YOU'RE TAKING OVER AN EXISTING TEAM?

Much of my discussion has focused on dealing with a team that you've been part of from the beginning. However, it's not that unusual for a leader to take over an existing team.

When this happens, the biggest mistake the leader can make is to charge in, guns blazing, ready to rearrange things so that they work the "right" way.

That existing group has a culture. Unless you disband the team and start over, you're going to have to deal with that culture. The bigger the organization you are taking over, the harder that is. It's one thing to disband a team of four or five, but harder to disband a company.

Take the time to understand how people on the team work. Speak to members and find out what's been successful and what hasn't. See if you can find out why they work the way they do. Periodically review the strategies we've discussed and the different emotions, and apply them. Invite feedback from your new team, request their help, and actually listen! Be patient. The process may go very quickly, or it may take some time. The only guarantee is that if you rush, it takes longer.

Review Quiz

1. The five bases of power are
   a. Legitimate, reward, coercive, information, referent
   b. Legitimate, coercive, information, expert, referent
   c. Wind, water, coal, oil, nuclear
   d. Legitimate, reward, coercive, expert, information
   e. Legitimate, reward, coercive, expert, referent
2. Which of the following statements is true?
   a. A team needs to be either all "I" or have no "I."
   b. There is no "I" in "team."
   c. The strength of the team comes through submerging individuality.

d. The strength of the individual comes only through complete autonomy.

e. The strength of the individual is the team; the strength of the team is the individual.

3. The emotion to minimize in team development is

a. Autonomy

b. Affiliation

c. Competence

d. Fear

e. There is no room for emotion in team development.

8

MANAGEMENT JUJITSU: NEGOTIATION, PROBLEM-SOLVING, AND DECISION-MAKING TECHNIQUES

O ne of the most important lessons in jujitsu is that of not using force. If someone wants to punch you in the face, you don't oppose him. You recognize his deep need to place his fist where your face is, and you politely move out of the way. If there happens to be a wall behind your head, it's not your fault if the attacker punches that wall. Indeed, it's not at all unlikely that your attacker will punch that wall extremely hard, with potentially detrimental effects on his fist.

If you tried to force him to punch that wall, you couldn't do it. He would fight you every step of the way. Even if you pointed a gun at him, it's unlikely he would hit the wall as hard as if he did it of his own free will. If you do try to force someone to punch a wall, you can expect that person's resistance to be exhausting, bruising, and unpleasant.

THE ART OF NONRESISTANCE

When I give this example in a talk, someone always points out that there's a big difference between punching a wall and building a product or working with a customer. Leaving aside the point that the latter two can often be like banging one's head against a wall, the real key is this: when you try to force someone to do something, he or she will resist, even to the point of resisting when you are trying to make that person do something that he or she originally wanted to do. The very fact that you are using force triggers people to assume that there must be some reason to fight back.

That person trying to punch you in the face has a vision. His vision involves his fist hitting your face. It may not be a vision that you, personally, agree with, but he has a vision. That's what makes it possible for you to allow him to punch the wall.

Now, the vision you are building for your employees is not destructive. It is, however, going to require some hard work, some serious time investment, and potentially some significant sacrifices on their part. If you have to force them to make that effort, you'll all find the process exhausting and unpleasant. Assuming that your goal is to run a successful team, produce products, serve customers, and get work done, this is not the way to go. Of course, if your goal is to win a fight in a highly inefficient manner, then maybe it is a good strategy.

Although I've never actually had someone try to punch me at the office, the process of being a manager is not unlike the practice of jujitsu. There will be times when you and your team disagree, members of the team disagree with one another, or you and your team disagree with other people in the company. Just like in the practice of jujitsu, you can oppose directly, or you can yield and let them have your way. In other words, you can negotiate.

Conflict is inevitable. How you handle it is up to you. You can attempt to squelch it, slapping down anyone who questions your authority or disagrees with you. At best, you will doom your team to minimal levels of performance. The Forming stage can last for years, especially if conflict is never permitted.

On the other extreme, you can engage in conflict with eagerness and gusto. You can make it clear to your team that they need to stand up and defend their positions and reward those who do it best. Every topic of disagreement becomes a battleground in which each person fights to prove the correctness of his ideas. Unfortunately, while this may be exciting for some people, it traps the team in the Storming phase. The environment can easily become toxic. It leaves people exhausted and burned out. You end up not with the best ideas but the loudest ones.

Negotiation is the process of managing that conflict. Properly harnessed and directed, conflict can yield excellent ideas. When questions are raised, people are able to argue back and forth and identify strengths and weaknesses of the ideas presented. Everything, including product design, work hours, work style, how to design the company logo, or how to run a meeting, can come up for debate as a team develops. You can waste that energy or you can focus it. You can create heroes eager for battle or a team that works together.

I am frequently told that negotiating means "giving in"—that not showing them (whomever "them" is) who is boss is a sign of weakness. Negotiating is no more giving in than dodging the fist and letting the attacker hit the wall is losing the fight. When you attempt to exert power over someone, it is human nature for that person to attempt to exert power to prevent you from doing it. Why fight? Why not let him have your way?

Fundamentally, any conversation, any interaction can become a negotiation. Whenever you want someone to do something that she isn't currently doing, whenever you ask someone to change her work style or approach, whenever you hire someone, whenever you do performance reviews—in all these instances, you are negotiating. You could be negotiating salary, overtime, scope of the project, vacation times, etc. It pays, therefore, to learn how to do it well.

The techniques I discuss here are heavily based on those developed by the Harvard Negotiation Project. If you want to study negotiation in greater depth, I recommend reading *Getting to Yes* by Roger Fisher and William Ury and *Getting Past No* by William Ury.

WHY DO YOU WANT WHAT YOU WANT?

You should never go into negotiations without understanding exactly what it is that you want out of the process. You also need to understand why you want what you want. What are your actual goals? If you don't correctly identify your goals, then you may find that you've won the negotiation and lost the war. You might have everything you asked for and nothing that you actually need.

Therefore, you need to spend some time understanding why it is you are negotiating. What are you really trying to accomplish? What, other than the obvious thing you're asking for, would satisfy you?

For example, let us suppose you have an employee who works odd hours, making it difficult to tell when she's in the office. One approach is to demand that she work nine to five like everyone else. That may not make sense, though; there may be a real reason for the odd hours, or perhaps you don't want to lose a good employee. Therefore, another approach is to identify the reasons why her schedule causes problems and see if you can address those problems directly. That would leave her autonomy intact, as well as her productivity. If, for instance, you discover that the problem is other employees don't know what she's doing, then the solution may be for you to create better communications between the team members. Perhaps you could, as many high-tech companies do, adopt a set of core hours and require that people be present during that time, which still leaves a great deal of flexibility.

Perhaps you're dealing with the manager of another department. The more the two of you need to work with one another, the more you need different ways of accomplishing your goals. It is a sad, but true, fact that no matter how important your goals are to you and no matter how important you believe they are to the company, the other guy may not agree. When you're dealing with a peer, you probably have no power over him. If the two of you can't reach agreement, the work won't get done. If you happen to be negotiating with a client, a vendor, or a competitor, the stakes are even higher and the use of power potentially more expensive.

It is wise to gain agreement ahead of time with the other parties involved on the rules and standards of your negotiation. In other words, how will you evaluate the final result? What metrics will you use to decide if it's worthwhile or not? If you're offering a new hire perks instead of salary, how will you both agree on relative value? If preexisting standards do not exist, then you'll need to develop them.

You might want to get someone to help you brainstorm different alternatives. He can also help you recognize when obsolete assumptions are getting in your way. For example, what if you have a highly productive employee who is working less than forty hours in a week? Is that even a problem? I can't count the number of times I've heard someone complain about an employee who is massively productive in less than forty hours while praising someone who is half as productive in fifty. What is your real problem here?

Identify what is really going on. How many different ways can you succeed? The more options you can come up with, the more likely you are to reach a good solution.

SURGERY IS A FORM OF MEDICINE

Some years ago, an extremely skilled jujitsu practitioner commented that when someone attacks him, he views that person as ill and his assault as a way of asking for help. He views it as his obligation to heal the attacker. He then added, "Surgery is a form of medicine." In other words, while he is willing to try to avoid the fight or attempt to end the fight without hurting his attacker, his fallback position is to make sure that he doesn't get hurt even if that means injuring or killing the attacker.

Know Your BATNA

There is a similar concept in negotiations. You never want to end a negotiation worse off than if you hadn't negotiated. The Harvard Negotiation Project calls this knowing your BATNA (Best Alternative to Negotiated Agreement). Your BATNA is the best you can do if the other side won't play ball. Any deal you make should be better than your BATNA or you are wasting your time. Because my students often have problems with this concept, I finally told them that a BATNA exists to prevent a Really Odious Blunder in Negotiations (ROBIN), and they needed to remember BATNA and ROBIN. That seemed to get results, although I don't know whether it was because of my clever acronym or because they were afraid I'd repeat the joke.

When negotiating with other people at the office, it's important to understand what their, and your, options are. What will they do if things don't go their way? How will they feel about it? If you're trying to hire someone, her BATNA might be to keep looking if she doesn't like your offer. If she has another job offer in hand, that strengthens her position.

If you're negotiating with someone on another team or with another manager, it's particularly important to understand what you can do without this person's help. Otherwise, you may find yourself committed to a delivery schedule that is going to leave you and your team burned out and still not get you what you wanted. If you are negotiating with a vendor, you need to understand your options lest you find yourself unable to purchase a component that you need.

Always identify your BATNA *before* you start talking to the other person. If you realize that a simple request just turned into a negotiating session, find some excuse to take a break and continue later. If you try to figure out your BATNA on the fly, you're much more likely to be caught up in the moment and make a mistake.

A final point: lest you believe that your BATNA should always be to find some compromise, please recognize that sometimes your BATNA is to go it alone and not hire the candidate, not give the raise, or not cooperate with the other company.

The Anger Response

In fencing, one of the best ways to beat someone is to get him angry. The problem with anger is that it narrows perceptions and decreases creativity. We become less able to anticipate consequences and, thus, plan for the future. We become increasingly reactive. Strategy goes out the window.

Once upon a time, there was a team. It was a strong, effective team—the sort of team that got things done. One day, two very prominent, leading members of this team disagreed on how things should be done. Over time, the disagreement became more and more intense. Instead of focusing on the good of the team, each leader slowly but inexorably became consumed with proving to the other that she was wrong. Some employees sided with one leader, some with the other. Eventually, one leader left with her followers to found another company. The other leader proudly proclaimed victory.

It was not long before both companies were out of business. Victory was expensive.

In a different situation, the new CEO took over a company. He didn't like the way things had been done under the previous regime. He was going to make some changes. The company would no longer tolerate the loose, somewhat freewheeling, disregard for the rules that the previous CEO had allowed. There would be structure. The company would run by the book. The stricter the CEO became, the more employees resisted or found ways to undermine the rules. Eventually, those who did not like the way things were being done were reminded that they could take advantage of this thing called a door.

The door got a lot of use. Even the traffic jam as everyone tried to fit through it at once didn't appreciably slow the exodus. When things finally settled down, the CEO, in a moment of extreme cliché, said, "Guess I showed them who's boss!"

Anger is a normal response when one is challenged or feeling threatened. It's just not the *best* response. An important part of negotiating is to give yourself space. Ury and Fisher describe this as "going to the balcony."

The key is to recognize that the threats are never so immediate as they seem. In a fight, it's hard to stop and think without getting hit. In an office, it's only our imaginations that prevent us from stopping and taking a break when tempers get hot or when we feel threatened or perceive that an employee is questioning our authority. The martial artist who allows his emotions to run away with him and becomes emotionally engaged in the conflict has one outcome: he loses. The manager, president, or CEO who becomes emotionally engaged in a conflict has two outcomes: you lose, in which case you've lost, or you win, in which case you've lost. The two team leaders and the CEO I mentioned earlier "won" their fights.

Fortunately, the lack of immediate, physical danger means that it's also not as hard to learn how to keep your cool under pressure. Unfortunately, our bodies react to financial or social threat much as they do to physical threat: we get angry, our hearts start pounding, and our bodies go into overdrive.

Therefore, the first, and perhaps most important, step is to remember that the apparent threat is an illusion. Your body may be telling you that you're in physical danger, but in reality, you have time to consider your responses. Call a break, drink some water, exercise, whatever it takes to give you some perspective.

Next, study your own reactions. What sets you off? How do you know when you're getting upset? Become aware of your triggers so that you can act preemptively if someone is trying to push those buttons.

Finally, maintain a sense of humor. A well-timed joke can relax the tension and let you get control of yourself and the situation, as well as demonstrate that you are not angry.

DO I SEE WHAT YOU SEE?

It's extremely difficult to fight someone when she is standing next to you and you are both looking in the same direction. It is very easy to fight with someone when you are facing her. It doesn't much matter whether we're talking about verbal or physical combat. In any sort of negotiation, it helps to look at things from the other person's point of view, to stand next to her and transform the negotiation into a process of joint problem solving. Ury and Fisher, quite aptly, call this "step to their side."

When you are negotiating, you are effectively in a team situation. That team is probably going to be in the Forming stage unless you are dealing with members of your own team, in which case you are at whatever stage the larger team has achieved. In other words, if your team has achieved Storming, then your interactions with any individual member of the team will be in Storming.

If you are negotiating with someone else, with your boss, with a peer, or with someone in another company, the "team" of the two (or more) of you may remain in Forming, or it may evolve. Being aware of that evolution will help you to manage the process and continually "step to their side."

Physical position actually does matter. When you sit across a table staring at someone, it's easy for the conversation to become adversarial. When you sit side-by-side or kitty-corner to the other person, it's easier to frame the situation as engaging in joint problem solving. Also, when someone expects conflict and you give cooperation, it takes that person mentally off-balance. That gives you an advantage.

Start by recognizing that you probably don't have all the facts. Even if you think you do, your employee, peer, vendor, or boss probably thinks that you don't. The fact is, it's very hard to know what you don't know. What to do?

Ask. The more open-ended the questions, the better. Avoid asking yes/no questions; they provide less information than you'd think, and they close off further discussion. When you ask someone if there's a problem, they will often say "no." Yet, they're still obviously not happy. When you ask someone, "What's getting in the way?" or "What do you see as the goal of this meeting?" you're going to get a more detailed answer, one that will give you useful information. By asking questions with a spirit of genuine inquiry, not sarcasm, you also further build the relationship between you and the person with whom you're speaking. Asking questions implicitly acknowledges the other's competence.

As the other person speaks, look for points of agreement. That doesn't mean you have to agree with her overall position, but you can frequently build affiliation by finding things that you can agree with. When someone says, "I'm extremely upset that we're being treated unfairly," you can respond with, "I'd also be upset if I felt I was being treated unfairly." You haven't agreed that the person is being treated unfairly but have merely recognized that you'd also be upset if it happened to you. The more small agreements you can reach, the stronger your position becomes. If necessary, start by agreeing just on a time and place for the meeting or what you'll order for lunch! Finding points of agreement builds affiliation and recognizes autonomy.

As the conversation progresses, periodically reflect back what you hear. That helps establish affiliation and demonstrates that you are paying attention:

Employee: "I've been spending so much time here that my family doesn't even recognize me!"
You: "Sounds like you feel you've been working pretty hard."

You are not making judgments, nor are you agreeing that the person shouldn't be working hard. What you are doing is acknowledging his status and building affiliation by showing that you're paying attention and processing what you're hearing. You are giving him an opportunity to correct any misapprehensions on your part. You are respecting his position and the power that he brings to the table. You might have legitimate power, but he might have expert power. As you use the conversation to build affiliation, you are also increasing your referent power: he will see your handling of the situation as respectful of him, and that will build your reputation as a manager who listens and treats people fairly. You will also, through practice, build your expert power.

Finally, take the time to periodically summarize what you hear. It can be particularly useful to summarize, ask for confirmation, and then end with a leading question:

You: "If I understand the situation correctly, you feel that the problem with the software is an unavoidable consequence of the platform we're using. Is that correct?"
Employee: "Yes."
You: "And if we go down this path, we're going to have a product that crashes when the customer tries to set a font size of 12 point. Is that correct?"
Employee: "Yes."
You: "What do you think we should do about this?" or "How do you feel we should explain this to the customer?"

Now, it's entirely possible that the person will refuse to engage in the conversation, in which case you may be forced to resort to your BATNA. However, it's also possible that you'll find out that the problem isn't what you think it is, or he'll come up with a solution, or both.

REFRAME OR REDIRECT CHALLENGES

If someone is trying to push your buttons, it's likely because she has a lot of respect for your abilities. Once again, avoid meeting force with force. When someone says, "That can't possibly work!" responding with "Oh yes, it can!"

or "It had better!" is directly opposing, or pitting your power against her power. No matter who wins, you both lose. Instead, ask, "Why not?" If her explanation doesn't make sense, ask her to clarify what she means. Quite frequently, the act of explaining will also help clarify the problem and lead to possible solutions.

Asking someone for her advice and suggestions is a powerful technique, and one that can be used in many situations. It's particularly useful when someone tells you that you don't know what you're talking about: "You might be right. What would you do in my place?"

Few people can resist the expert role. When you give them an opportunity to expound on their point of view, they'll usually take it. Not only does that get you useful information, it helps build autonomy and competence. It gives you the opportunity to help them see things from your perspective; you are turning the conversation from argument to joint problem solving. At the same time, look for opportunities to see things from their perspective. The more you demonstrate you see where they are coming from, the more acceptable the results of the negotiation.

THE PATH OF LEAST RESISTANCE

Part of the principle of not meeting force with force in jujitsu is never compelling an attacker to fall down. Rather, one should make it easy for the opponent to fall and then get out of his way. The jujitsu practitioner does not force an attacker to punch a wall but simply makes it easy for him to do so. By the same token, you want to avoid forcing someone to accept the results of a negotiation. Rather, you want to make it easy for people to go where you would like them to go. Ury and Fisher refer to this step as "building a golden bridge."

In order to build the path of least resistance, make your vision of the future so attractive that people will want to go there. Just as when you're building a vision for the company or the team, so are you helping an individual see how his or her personal vision fits into the larger vision. Don't try to do it all yourself: invite his input. Give her every opportunity to help paint that attractive future. The more involved people are, the more ownership they'll take. The more ownership they take, the easier it is for them to want to go to that future.

As you build the vision, ask others for their advice on how to get there. Once again, that puts them in the expert role and gets them invested in the process. It builds affiliation, since they are contributing, and competence, since they are now the expert. Apply reverse goal-chaining: keep walking them backward until you reach the current situation. Ask them what needs to happen in order for them to take that first step. Specifically, find out what obstacles are in their way and then brainstorm ways to remove those obstacles.

Sometimes, you believe you've created that path of least resistance, and yet the other person stubbornly refuses to go along it. Don't push him. Slow down. In jujitsu, speed comes from moving at the pace of your attacker. If you rush, you lose. Find out what's going on. There's probably a reason he doesn't want to take the first step. Is he afraid of losing face? If so, help him save face. Is he concerned that he isn't getting something he needs? Figure out a way to give him something that lets him feel satisfied. Don't assume a fixed pie or a zero-sum game. There are often things you can offer that are cheap for you and valuable to the other party. See what you can come up with.

Recognize that if someone hasn't bought into the vision or doesn't see you as an ally, he probably won't trust that easy path. In that case, you need to work on building more affiliation with him. Look for opportunities to build affiliation by showing appreciation or finding common ground.

If he's feeling forced, he might refuse to take the step because you're infringing on his autonomy. Reduce the pressure. Make it his idea.

Avoid getting into a "Come on, only an idiot couldn't see this!" mindset. That's stepping on his sense of competence. You may find an attitude of, "This isn't easy, but I'm betting you can handle it," to be more productive. When you appeal to someone's competence and expertise, you are more likely to get results than when you question that competence and expertise.

Remember, your goal is not to stand on your opponent's foot while you try to throw him. Your goal is to make it easy for him to go where you want him to go.

USE THEIR IMAGINATIONS

A certain high-ranking jujitsu expert was accosted on the street. As the attacker approached, she said, "Wait a moment!" and did a flip, landing on her back on the sidewalk. She jumped to her feet with a big smile and said, "Ready!"

The attacker turned and ran.

The woman in this scenario made no threats. She didn't say, "Back off, I'm a fifth degree black belt." She simply gave an impromptu demonstration and then left the rest to the attacker's imagination. He very wisely remembered urgent business elsewhere. Had she been forced to fight, she might have been injured or faced legal consequences afterward. She not only avoided meeting force with force, she successfully used her knowledge and skill to convey to the attacker what could happen to him. She did what Ury and Fisher describe as "using power to educate."

Threats only trigger resistance. Attacking someone's autonomy leads them to exert that autonomy. By extension, when you make it difficult for someone to say no to you, you are also making it difficult for them to say yes—saying yes would involve a loss of face and an acceptance that he had been overpowered. No one likes being put in that position, and if your goal is any sort of long-term relationship with the other person, it's worth the effort to not put him there. People put in that position look for opportunities to strike back. There's nothing like having an employee accept a new job at exactly that moment when you need all hands on deck to really bring a warm feeling to your cheeks.

So don't make threats; use their imaginations. When you find people who are unwilling to cooperate, ask them, "What do you think I should do in this situation?" or "What do you suppose will happen if you go ahead with this course of action?" Look for opportunities to show people a glimpse of what could happen. Give them enough to get their imaginations going. Respect their autonomy and their competence by giving them the picture and letting them draw the appropriate conclusions.

Fighting all too often becomes lose-lose. Your goal is win-win.

FEEDBACK AND REVIEWS

At this point, let's look at a particularly vexing problem: the art of employee feedback and reviews. This topic was brought into sharp relief recently when someone came to me and said, "We were thinking of doing a 360-degree feedback to help him understand what other people think."

This very frustrated comment referred to efforts to explain to a very senior manager that his style of leadership wasn't working for his team. So far, all efforts to convince him to change were foundering on the simple perception that, from the manager's point of view, things were working just fine. That being the case, it's hard to imagine how a 360 would help. Sure, he might find that his subordinates don't much like him, but he might also feel that his job isn't to be liked, it's to get people to perform.

More broadly, it's important to recognize that there's nothing particularly special about 360-degree feedback. It's a tool. Like any tool, it's useful only if you know how to use it and if it's the right tool for the job. Before you can tell if it's the right tool, you first have to understand what the job is.

In this situation, the job is getting someone to accept feedback and then make use of that feedback to alter his behavior. In this way, giving feedback is a form of negotiation. At a very fundamental level, feedback is only useful if it gives people the information they need to change and provides them a rationale for why they should change. It helps considerably if the feedback also increases an employee's sense of competence and commitment to the goals of the team and the company. Remember the high-performance cycle: increased commitment leads to increased performance, and decreased commitment leads to decreased performance.

Now, I've certainly watched any number of managers take the attitude that their subordinates were going to change or leave. This is not particularly useful for either the employee or the team. It doesn't benefit anyone to have a disgruntled employee quit at a critical time in the life of a project, and the employee doesn't learn how to improve his performance. As a result, the team never achieves the level of performance it's capable of achieving. In terms of organizational behavior, we're looking at a direct application of coercive power, which leads to resistance and constant struggle. Even if you win, using force eventually leads to decreased commitment to the goals of the company.

Understanding Feedback

Before you can provide feedback, you must agree on what the feedback is going to be about. Clear goals must be established well in advance of any feedback. As obvious as this may sound, I had someone at one company tell me recently that she had no idea when she was ever going to get a performance review, but that was OK because she also had no idea on what criteria she would be evaluated. She figured she'd simply do her best and hope that things worked out in the end. Without goals, feedback is often arbitrary, little more than criticism and argument. You can't coach or motivate an employee when you haven't even agreed on what that employee should be doing!

Assuming that you have clear goals defined, feedback needs to be timely. The idea of doing feedback at six-month or one-year intervals is convenient, but of limited effectiveness. Few things are more infuriating to an employee than to be criticized over something that happened months before. Frequently, the employee doesn't remember the incident in question, but even worse is when it's a behavior he's been repeating because he didn't know he shouldn't. There are any number of ways for people to get timely feedback that don't involve a formal feedback session with a manager; it is well worth the time and effort to set those up. Possibilities include informal chats over lunch, going to the gym with an employee, and so forth. The more you've built affiliation and demonstrated your appreciation for your employees as people, the easier it is to give them feedback.

Respect Autonomy

One of the big criticisms I've heard from employees is that they feel powerless when they get a review. Making someone feel powerless is one of the best ways to get them to ignore what you are telling her or argue every step of the way. Fortunately, it's relatively easy to avoid this. Invite the employee to pick the time and date of the feedback session. Provide some choices, but try to let your employee choose. That simple act of giving her some power dramatically increases the probability that she will be receptive during the feedback session itself. You are actively promoting her autonomy and respecting her status on the team. If you manage people who are experts in a particular field, then it's particularly important to respect that expert power your employees bring to the table.

Be Specific

Another problem that I've run into repeatedly is that feedback can be so vague as to be useless. Vague goals yield vague focus; vague feedback yields confusion. Telling an employee that he is "too aggressive," or "not aggressive enough," is meaningless. Your definition of "aggressive" and your employee's definition may be completely different. In one company I worked with, the same employee was told by two managers that he was "too passive" because "he wouldn't argue for his position with the team" and "a good team player" because he was willing to "put his ego aside and work for the good of the team."

If you actually expect the employee to make a change in his behavior, or continue a behavior that you like, the trick is to make the feedback specific: "In the meeting the other day, I felt you had some very valid points and were too quick to give up on them," is far more useful than "You were too passive." Similarly, the following is far better than just telling someone that he's "a good team player": "I noticed the other day when you requested input from the rest of the team and used it to modify your suggestion. I really appreciated you setting an example of collaboration instead of competition on the team."

Going Negative

Another question is how to provide negative feedback. The key thing to recognize is that while you might see negative feedback as helping an employee improve her performance, the employee probably sees it just a little bit differently. She may well feel that her job is being threatened. Someone who feels threatened will not be receptive, so it's important to create an atmosphere conducive to presenting the information. It must be clear that you are trying to build the employee up, not tear her down. The stronger the relationship you have with your employees, the easier that will be. If you've been managing through fear, it will be harder, and your feedback will likely be ignored or resisted.

Many managers like to deal with negative feedback by slipping the negative comments in between two positive comments. That's fine, but you still have to make the feedback precise. In this case, it's even more critical to focus on specific behaviors in specific situations. As MIT's Ed Schein advises, avoid making generalizations about someone's motives, motivation, or personality. As soon as you tell someone that she "clearly doesn't want to do well," "clearly doesn't have what it takes," or "has a difficult personality," you are moving into the realm of criticizing unchangeable aspects of the person. That's neither useful nor productive and will only generate resistance. Instead, focus on exactly what the employee did and when she did it. Explain to her how you feel that her actions sent the wrong message. Focus on your perceptions and feelings; don't try to tell her what she was feeling. Take the time to understand exactly what the problem is. Don't make assumptions.

Build Up, Not Tear Down

Paradoxical as it may seem, the best way to improve the performance of someone who is not performing as well as desired is to find things to praise, not things to criticize. You still need to convey the problems but also take the time to build the person up. For example, the following feedback is not particularly useful or effective: "What is wrong with you? That project had nothing to do with our goals. Why did you waste your time and energy on that instead of working on something productive?" At best, it will decrease, if not destroy, the employee's motivation. The typical response to "What's wrong with you?" is a determined "Nothing!"

To build the employee up and increase his or her motivation, it helps to approach the situation a little differently: "I am concerned that you are not producing results at the rate we expected. I need to understand what is going on. What obstacles are you facing?" You'll notice that this example applies the negotiation techniques we discussed earlier in this chapter. You are asking genuine, open-ended questions designed to both elicit information and also build the employee's sense of autonomy. You are also communicating your concerns about the situation without making any judgments.

It's important to give the employee a chance to present his perception of what is going on. You might hear something unexpected, or he might have misunderstood his goals. This is not uncommon among newer employees, especially those fresh out of school. The trick is to focus them where you want them and give them the confidence to succeed: "While that project wasn't really appropriate to our goals, I really liked the way you approached it. You put an incredible amount of effort into it. You researched the information you needed, you spent the time necessary to carry it out. I have rarely seen that level of focus. How can I help you apply it to . . ."

If an employee is worth keeping, there is always something to praise. Make it specific, and tie it to the behaviors you want to see repeated. Invite the employee to participate in brainstorming with you to improve his performance. If necessary, conduct the conversation over lunch; changing the venue and adding a relaxed note helps stimulate creativity. Inviting him to help you help him increases his sense of personal control and hence his level of personal commitment to success. Transforming a negative into a positive is one of the most powerful techniques for increasing an employee's productivity, motivation, and commitment.

Remember Your Goals!

The goal of employee feedback is, most commonly, improving performance. Keep that in mind as you approach the review. Identify ahead of time what you want to accomplish and make sure you know how you'll know if you succeed. Also consider ahead of time how you'll handle an employee who refuses to change or adapt to different circumstances. If you allow yourself to become angry and make a decision in the heat of the moment, it'll probably be the wrong one.

Review Quiz

1. The phrase "surgery is a form of medicine" means
   a. You should always find a compromise
   b. Sometimes you walk away from the negotiation
   c. It's important to make sure the other side gets what they need
   d. You should fight tooth and nail for what you want
   e. Negotiation doesn't end until both parties are in the ER

2. In the course of negotiation, it is important to
   a. Be aware of your own emotional triggers
   b. See things from the other side's point of view
   c. Use their imagination
   d. Find the path of least resistance
   e. All of the above

3. In giving feedback, it is important to
   a. Set the time, place, and agenda and then tell your employee
   b. Establish clear goals ahead of time
   c. Meet no more often than once per year
   d. Find things to criticize so that employees don't get above themselves
   e. Never admit when someone does good work lest you have to pay that employee more

4. Negative feedback should be
   a. Focused on the defects in the employee's personality
   b. Broad and encompassing
   c. Accompanied by threats of what will happen if the employee doesn't improve
   d. Focused on events that happened months before
   e. Specific and detailed with a focus on your observations and reactions

5. The most common goal of feedback is to
   a. Enable the employee to improve performance
   b. Make the manager feel good
   c. Provide an excuse to avoid raises
   d. Put people in their place
   e. None of the above

9

MANAGING CHANGE

What do moving the coffeepot and altering the way an organization does business have in common? As anyone who has ever attempted even what appear to be minor changes to office routines has discovered, the prospect of change can provoke surprisingly strong negative reactions in many people. While the debate over the location of the coffeepot may resolve fairly quickly, at least once all concerned manage to become sufficiently caffeinated, other aspects of organizational change are not so easily handled.

A PARADIGM IS NOT TWENTY CENTS

You will recall that we briefly discussed change in Chapter 1 and touched on it again in Chapter 5 when talking about establishing office routines and the importance of shaking them up once in a while. Just to be perfectly clear, let me reiterate that while it can be useful to shake up routines occasionally, doing it frequently will negate the benefits of having a routine and leave people feeling constantly frustrated and confused. This chapter is not about making short-term, temporary changes to revitalize a stale routine or give people a break. This chapter is about making long-term, lasting changes in the way the organization works.

I frequently hear that people "do not like to change." However, that's not entirely true.

In reality, we change constantly. As we discussed in Chapter 1, organizations are always changing. It's not the change itself that most people object to. People object to being changed by someone else, and people object to change that comes too rapidly for them to adjust. When people feel like events are moving too fast for them, they instinctively dig in their heels and resist. Remember our discussions of affiliation and autonomy? Rapid change undermines autonomy and threatens to destroy affiliation with the image of the company.

This requires some further explanation.

Quite simply, people become attached to their jobs—not so much in a financial sense, but in an emotional one. Most people define themselves at least in part by what they do. Now this concept is probably not a big surprise. However, when there's a change at work, that change may touch on how people view themselves or how they view their jobs. While it is highly unlikely that many people define themselves by the location of the coffeemaker, the problem is that it's very hard to determine exactly what it is that someone finds important. Even apparently minor or benign changes can trigger fear and anxiety as people start to worry about some or all of these questions:

- **What will this do to the organization?** In other words, will I still feel that this is a company where I am proud to be an employee?
- **How will my place in the organization change?** I know what I'm doing now. Will I still know what I'm doing after the change? Will I be able to handle the work? Will I lose status as a result of the change?
- **Will this affect my job?** Will I still have a job I care about after the changes are complete? Will I be laid off/downsized/euphemized in some other way?
- **Will I still enjoy working here?** Will the things that make working here fulfilling still be in place?
- **Will this hurt our product quality?** In other words, might this change threaten the viability of the organization, and hence my livelihood and career?
- **Will I still measure up?** I can't tell if I'd be viewed as competent in the brave new world!
- **Would I be able to get a job in this new organization?** Oh my god, I won't be qualified to work here once the changes are complete! They're going to replace me with someone cheaper!

Recall that a job is, to many people, more than just a paycheck. As we discussed in Chapter 4, a job offers people an environment where they can apply their skills on something that, hopefully, matters to them. The job is a source of identity, status, purpose, and security. If they've bought in to your vision, then the job represents part of their vision of their future. Changes threaten not just what is, but what will be.

When you seek to make lasting changes to the workplace, you are altering something that people view as solid as the ground under their feet. Having lived in California during the Loma Prieta earthquake, I know what a very unsettling experience that is. The effects don't necessarily go away immediately afterward either. The first time after the quake that the cat jumped on the bed in the middle of the night, I just about jumped through the roof. If there were an Olympic medal for highest jump from a prone position, I would have been a serious contender. This is how people feel about organizational change, only more so. Organizational change is more pervasive and longer lasting, and it's harder to see the full extent of it.

Another problem is that these questions may not come up directly; rather, they may manifest as debate about whether or not the values of the business are being honored, questions about the validity of the changes, etc. Other times, the questions may manifest in a passive refusal to change, or in a constant tendency to "forget" and slip back into the old way of doing things in order to wear down management. Sometimes this works.

In one situation, the manager of an engineering team was quietly undermined and driven out by the team; there was no open, planned rebellion, but rather the manager simply became exhausted fighting his team's gravitational attraction to the "old way." Prior to Lou Gerstner taking over at IBM, numerous attempts at organizational change were swallowed by IBM's corporate equivalent of the La Brea tar pits.

I worked with one software organization where we needed to change the way defects were tracked and reported to engineering. The assurances that the new process would be easier, take less time than the old one, and result in a higher quality product didn't matter. Even the fact that a weekly, all-day bug tracking meeting was eliminated and replaced with a brief status meeting didn't matter. What mattered to people was that something that they saw as inviolate was being changed, and thus their whole image of the company was being changed as well. Engineering had always had the final say over which bugs were fixed and who fixed them. Changing that caused the engineers to feel that their competence was being questioned and autonomy threatened. The initial response was one of continual, passive resistance.

Dealing with that resistance involved helping all parties recognize that they all had the same goals for the company, the product, and each person's ability to manage his or her own time. It meant addressing fears, rational and irrational. Once it became clear that the goal wasn't to assign blame but to enhance the customer experience without increasing demands on engineering, the engineering team became an enthusiastic supporter of the new process.

What each of the questions about change really represents is an inability to see the future. While that may seem to be a silly statement—in that none of us can actually see the future—the problem is that the future that you can't see is extremely discomforting.

Confronted with the prospect of change, there is a window of opportunity during which people take in the news and evaluate the situation. During that window, most people are initially ambivalent. It's when they are told how great the change will be, how there's nothing to worry about, and how they should just go along because there really isn't any choice that they start resisting. When people are trying to make up their minds how they feel about something, pushing them tends to produce an immediate, and opposing, reaction: we instinctively defend our autonomy. Remember our discussion of negotiation? When you make it hard for someone to say "no," you also make it hard for them to say "yes."

So how do you defuse this natural resistance before it becomes active or passive rebellion or a mass exodus of employees? The key is to recognize a couple of things: first, resistance is a sign that you are going too fast, and second, people are generally quite willing to change themselves.

HOW DO I BUILD MOMENTUM FOR CHANGE?

The key is to move at the appropriate speed and let people change themselves. As we discussed in the previous chapter, your goal is not to force people to do things your way but to let them have your way. Just as with any form of motivation, you want to create an organization that knows where to go and will trample anyone and anything that gets in its way. You don't do that through force; you do it through leadership.

How Do I Start?

A moment ago, I wrote that the future you can't see is very discomforting. Lacking a clear image of the future, people seem to be more likely to project a negative future than a positive one. Indeed, both the stock market and politics demonstrate how hard it is to sell a positive future and how easily people tend to assume the worst in the absence of a strong positive message.

You need to start, therefore, by creating that strong, positive message. You may wish to review the discussion of vision in Chapter 3.

Your vision for the future of the organization needs to show people a positive, optimistic future that will result from the changes you are advocating. Members of the organization need to at least tentatively buy into that future first, before you do anything else. This is an example of the reverse goal-chaining technique. It's important to demonstrate confidence in your vision of the future while at the same time expressing your concern about what will happen if nothing is done. Don't go overboard here; your goal is not to get people to panic but to get them to think and to imagine that things really could work out well for them and for the company.

Part of your vision must acknowledge the concerns people will inevitably have and seek to directly or indirectly allay those concerns.

As part of constructing your vision, you need to consider how you can use it to build people's sense of competence, affiliation, and autonomy. Remember that fear undermines affiliation, so look for ways to reduce fear and focus affiliation on the company of the future. Look for ways to create a future in which people know that they will be competent. Seek opportunities to give your employees autonomy in how they move toward that future. In short, you need to build motivation and excitement around the changes.

How Do I Convince My Employees That the Vision Is Their Vision?

Actively seek out opportunities to get your employees involved in shaping the vision of the future. However, don't force it. Invite, invite, and then invite some more.

At one company, each employee was ordered to come up with two ideas to move the company forward. While that may sound like a great way to include everyone, in fact it was seen as just another way to undermine autonomy and get people to eliminate themselves. Leave the door open, invite opinions, and recognize that enthusiasm takes time to build.

Brainstorm with employees on how to change and what changes will be best. Forge agreement on the ultimate goals of the change process. Treat objections as opportunities to develop innovative solutions, not as signs of argument or disloyalty.

How Fast Should I Go?

Recognize that resistance is not something to smash through. Resistance is a signal that you are moving too quickly. Slow down and acknowledge employee concerns; don't try to minimize or ignore them. That only sends the message that the concern must be really serious because you aren't willing to discuss it. Acknowledging their concerns also helps reinforce the feeling that you're all in this together. Quietly reinforcing a sense of community is critical in reassuring people that you really do have their interests at heart.

Speed is, fundamentally, an illusion. You go the fastest by being in the right place at the right time. That requires spending the time to know where and when the right place and the right time are. If you just rush forward, first, it can be extremely difficult to keep everyone moving together, and second, you may just find that you've missed your goal. Rushing around and not accomplishing anything, or worse, accomplishing the wrong thing, undermines your credibility and uses up time and energy.

You do not want to spend your time constantly circling back to redirect groups that have stopped moving or even started retreating to the status quo. Change fails when you force people to move forward. At that point you're in the business of herding cats. Change succeeds when people move forward because they want to.

How Do I Build Motivation for Change?

While building motivation for change starts with a compelling vision, that vision is only a start. As part of communicating that vision, you have the opportunity to enable your employees to convince themselves that the change is both necessary and beneficial to their future careers. Considering everything we've covered to this point, how might you do that?

If you said, "by asking questions," you'd be correct. You need to ask the sort of open-ended questions that will enable people to convince themselves of the following:

- Change is necessary.
- Change is positive.
- They are capable of making change happen.
- They know what to do to make the change happen.

In order to create the mindset that change is necessary, start by asking about the status quo. For example, you might ask these questions:

- What would happen if we did nothing?
- How is the current situation holding you back?
- What worries you about the current situation?
- Why do you suppose we need to do something?

You'll notice that none of these are yes/no questions. Each question forces the person to consider his answer and frame the response in terms of what you need him to be saying. As the old saying goes, "The more I talk, the more I know what I believe." You want to get people talking about the status quo in dissatisfied terms. The more your employees become dissatisfied with the way things are, the easier it is to get them focused on the way things could be.

The next step is to focus people on the idea that change is a good thing, a positive thing. Having made them unhappy with the way things are, you now need to start getting them excited about doing something about it. It's time to start asking questions that highlight the advantages of change:

- How would you like things to be different?
- What would be good about the team working together better?
- What would be the advantage to you of making a change?
- How could a change make us more competitive?
- What opportunities would change open up for you?

You'll notice the mix of questions about the individual and about the company. You want people to feel that the company's future is their future and their future dreams and hopes will be realized by supporting the company.

The goal of these questions is to get people talking about change as a good thing, as a solution to the problems of the present. You've helped them identify the problems of the status quo, and now you've helped them recognize that a solution is possible, that things could be better. The next step is to enable them to realize that they can make change happen. Nothing succeeds like the expectation of success. The next set of questions needs to focus on building up that optimistic, can-do attitude that will leave people expecting to succeed:

- What makes you think that if you did decide to change, you could do it?
- Have you ever made a significant change like this before? How did you do it?
- What strengths do you/the team/the company have that would help make this work?

You'll note that these questions focus purely on the reasons why change can work, not the reasons why it can't. You don't want to spend your time asking people for all the reasons change might fail. That focuses them on failure. Instead, you want them to recite their strengths and remember any relevant previous successes. Again, the process is one of building people up. You want the people in your organization to tackle change like Lance Armstrong biking up a mountain: with complete focus and an unwavering belief in their own inevitable success.

Once you've built up that expectation of success, it's time to get people moving. If you don't do anything, the excitement will fade away and be replaced by pessimism. You need to get people started and give them some initial successes to cement their confidence and enable them to prove to themselves that they can do it. Again, you enable your employees to tell you what needs to happen next:

- So what do you intend to do?
- Forget about "how"—what do you want to have happen?
- What will tell us we're getting started?
- What will tell us we're making progress?

Whether or not you get detailed action plans, what you will get are strong intentions to move forward. Your employees will be brainstorming with you on how to make change happen. They are involved and actively committed to the process.

Now you have to keep the momentum going and help it to build upon itself. Periodically summarize the feedback you are getting from your employees. Echo it back to them, and check to make sure that they are still in agreement. If not, adjust as necessary to bring people back on board and keep their enthusiasm high. Make sure they know that you see what they see, and help them to see what you see.

Whether you ask these questions from the front of a lecture hall, in small group meetings, or even one-on-one with key managers and employees, you need to listen to the responses. If you want to stand on a podium, great! Just be sure there's some way for dialogue to occur. If the company is large, you may not be able to do it all yourself. That's fine; start by recruiting key people into the change process and have them spread the word to their people.

Once you've done all that, you are ready to implement active change in your organization. The next step is to make change as easy as possible. As we discussed in the last chapter, your goal at this point is to make the path of change the path of least resistance.

HOW DO I MAKE CHANGE EASY?

Part of making change easy is to go back and review the underlying "resistance" questions:

- What will this do to the organization?
- How will my place in the organization change?
- Will this affect my job?
- Will I still enjoy working here?
- Will this hurt our product quality (threaten the organization)?
- Will I still measure up?
- Would I be able to get a job in this new organization?

We've started to deal with these issues by helping employees answer questions designed to increase motivation and confidence around change. Now we have to create the structure that will make change the path of least resistance.

Help Them Measure Up

When the Boston Celtics develop a new play, their coach tells them what to do, and then they get right out on the basketball court and do it perfectly in competition the first time.

Well, maybe not.

In fact, when you look at any successful athlete or athletic team, you rarely, if ever, see them trying to execute a new play in competition without having rehearsed it at length ahead of time. No matter how skilled they are, they put in that practice time. Indeed, one of the biggest differences between top performers and average ones is that the former put in the time it takes to train. In the end, it doesn't matter how much you may want to succeed if you aren't willing to make the effort to prepare.

Making any nontrivial change in your organization works the same way. People do not just reset habits and routines that have become familiar through long practice. The motivation, willingness, and confidence to change that you've built is wonderful, but habits are hard to change no matter how motivated we are to do it.

Fortunately, the goal is not to break the old habits but to create new ones. Breaking a habit is extremely difficult. Creating a new habit is much, much easier if it's done right.

This is the point at which the leadership must demonstrate that they are serious about making the change work. Their actions and their commitment at this point will determine how successful change is going forward.

You demonstrate that the leadership embraces the change by training people in the new ways of doing things. Whether or not you provide the time and money to prepare people will send a clear message to your organization about how seriously you take the change process. If you skimp at this point, then you risk being seen as all talk, no action.

It is particularly important that you train your organization by group, not by individual. Training needs to respect and reinforce the bonds of affiliation that you've already built. If you try to train individual members of a group as a pilot project or cost saving or whatever, it generally will not work because you are compromising the individual's affiliation with the rest of his or her coworkers. People who work as a team must be trained as a team in the new ways of working.

Training as a team offers several critical advantages.

First and foremost, training together as a team reinforces affiliation. The team is not just learning the new methodologies and procedures, they are learning to perform them with one another. Just like athletes in spring training, employees need to become comfortable with how each of them approaches the new material. They need to reset and reconstruct all of those implicit assumptions and routines that they've built to date.

You'll recall from Chapter 1 that culture is very hard to change. Cultural values are tangled together and mutually reinforcing. When you don't address the interplay between people, in other words, the cultural habits and assumptions, you are leaving the old values as a constant, default behavior. Under stress, default behaviors are the most likely to emerge. If those behaviors are not changed then, given enough time, your change efforts will gradually slide back to where you started.

The next major advantage to training as a team is that team members will be able to help and reinforce one another. As the new procedures are learned, members can assist each other and remind each other to practice. This speeds up adoption and increases retention of the new information.

Of course, when you're training a team, you need a trainer or, if you prefer, a coach. That could be the manager, if that manager has the appropriate skills, or it could be someone else. If it's someone else, the manager of the team must participate in the training with the team. Leaders are members first. If the leader doesn't train with the members, adoption of new material, methods, techniques, etc., is hampered or blocked completely. Ed Schein points out in his book *Helping* that teams in which leaders do not train with the rest of the membership often never master new techniques or ways of doing business.

How Do I Get to Carnegie Hall?

A key part of training is practice. No one learns anything nontrivial by just being told. People need to rehearse until the new behaviors start to feel natural. Whether you're bringing in a new bug-tracking system or converting from paper to electronic forms, you need to give people the time they need to learn the new material and become comfortable with it. That may mean accepting that less work will get done while the new techniques are being absorbed. Recognize that if you try to cram in too much, you simply increase the stress level, which strengthens old behaviors and makes it harder to learn new skills. Provide opportunities and venues for new skills to be practiced. This may be easy if you're changing something small or that provides a natural practice setting. It may be difficult if your changes are complex and far reaching. What is important is that employees need a place to experiment, explore, and become comfortable with the new ways of working. They need to be able to ask questions without feeling stupid, and they need to be able to make mistakes without fear of punishment. They need to be able to vent and express their natural frustrations with the situation and their progress. It's best to provide the opportunity to vent with outsiders or with some form of moderator so that the venting doesn't turn into an echo chamber that blocks progress.

Remember, you don't just want your employees to learn the material. You want them to *overlearn* the material. It needs to become automatic, something they'll do without thinking about it. It needs to become the new routine.

Show the End First

A mystery novel is fun because we don't know how it'll turn out. Trying to figure out whodunit is part of the fun.

Don't make organizational change into a mystery novel.

Show people what the results of the process will look like. We've already discussed one aspect of this when we discussed building a vision of change. It's also important to show people how the business will work afterward. If the changes you are making have already been successfully accomplished in one part of the organization, communicate that. Let everyone else see the success and what that success looks like. Create role models so that employees have visible successes to imitate and people to identify with.

If your organizational change is sufficiently large and no part of your business has yet implemented it, then you might want to make a professionally produced video showing people how the business will work once the changes are complete. A picture is worth a thousand words. Besides, the act of creating the "prototype" might just alert you to problems that you didn't foresee.

Provide Multiple Avenues

Different people learn in different ways. It is extremely helpful to provide multiple methods of instruction whenever possible and allow people to choose. By providing choices, you are maximizing autonomy, which, in turn, maintains and increases motivation.

Look for ways of making the different training methods fun. The simple reality is that people learn best when they are enjoying themselves. The more unpleasant it is to learn something new, the less likely it is that the material will actually be learned.

I've found that one of the best learning environments for many situations is complex, highly detailed, serious role-playing games, also known as *predictive scenarios*. The games must be sufficiently complex to not be boring and sufficiently immersive to cause appropriate behaviors to emerge. For more information on this topic, see my chapter "Reality from Fantasy: Using Predictive Scenarios to Explore Ethical Dilemmas" in *Ethics and Game Design: Teaching Values Through Play*, edited by Karen Schrier and David Gibson.

WHAT ABOUT FEEDBACK?

As with any other goal, make sure that employees have easy access to feedback. They need to know how they're doing and if they're doing the right thing. Make a point of praising the new behaviors whenever you see them. You don't have to make a big deal of it, but you do need to let people see that you care.

Recall from our discussion of culture that one of the most powerful tools a leader has at her disposal is the choice of where to focus people's attention. What you demonstrate that you care about is what people will take seriously. What you praise is what will be repeated. What you ignore is what will fade away.

Another effective technique is to occasionally reward groups that have made significant accomplishments in bringing about change. There are a couple of ways to do this. The best is to take the opportunity to celebrate significant milestones. Major changes can be draining on an organization, so it's worthwhile to take the time to pause periodically, review the progress you've been making, and recharge your batteries. Don't minimize the accomplishments; this reduces self-efficacy and feelings of competence. Rather, recognize how difficult it was and use that difficulty to maximize the sense of accomplishment. The more successful people feel they've been, the more successful they will be going forward.

Thus, avoid statements like, "Well, you've done well so far, but it hasn't even gotten difficult yet. The really hard part is yet to come." A statement like that is not one that gets people all excited and eager to tackle the next challenge.

Instead, say something along the lines of, "We've hit our first milestone. I can tell from the long hours and hard work you all put in that it wasn't easy. Frankly, I'm impressed at how rapidly you did it. You exceeded my most optimistic expectations."

What you've done with this second statement is focus on the hard work and dedication that people put in. You've recognized it, praised it, and implicitly acknowledged the efforts and sacrifices that your employees are making. You've also built up their sense of competence by telling them how well they did. You'll recall the concept of comparing people favorably to the nonexistent other. By telling them they beat your mental image of how long it would take, you've just raised their own perceptions of their abilities.

If you can add a statement along the lines of "We are now 10 percent (or 20 percent or whatever percent) done!" so much the better. It's always more motivating to be reminded of how much you've done rather than how much there is yet to do.

Above all, make sure that you are living up to the changes yourself. If you've imposed a penalty for not living up to a change, then make sure you honor that penalty should you slip and make a mistake. For example, at one company, the manager of the group became frustrated with meetings always starting late. He imposed a twenty-five cent penalty anytime someone arrived late to a meeting. That money would go to buying donuts or pizza periodically. A week or two after imposing this rule, he was late for the meeting. His staff gleefully demanded that he pay up. After a moment of stunned silence, he laughed and tossed a quarter into the kitty. Compliance increased dramatically thereafter.

You'll notice, by the way, that the penalty for noncompliance was not severe. It was purely symbolic. When it comes to negative feedback, ninety-nine times out of a hundred, that's really all you need—a quiet method of letting someone know that he's off track without being punitive or embarrassing. At the risk of being repetitive, people must feel they have the freedom to make mistakes if you want them to learn new behaviors. The feedback for those mistakes does not need to be and should not be severe. It should just be enough to let them know they're moving off track.

THE SECRET TO SUCCESSFUL CHANGE

The key to remember is that successful change doesn't come from fear or speed. It comes from helping people to see that the change will make their lives and their work experience better, not worse. It comes from building optimism and belief in the change process. In short, it comes from building competence. The faster you move, the slower you go.

Review Quiz

1. Even an apparently benign change to the company can trigger which of the following questions?
   a. Where will the coffeepot end up?
   b. Will I have to get a new suit?
   c. Why can't they make up their minds?
   d. How will my place in the organization change?
   e. What shall we have for lunch?
2. Minimizing employee concerns about change
   a. Is the best way to move things forward
   b. Implicitly acknowledges that employees care
   c. Saves managers valuable time and prevents whining
   d. Implies that the concerns are too difficult to be addressed
   e. None of the above
3. In order to convince employees that change is necessary, you should
   a. Ask questions
   b. Give speeches
   c. Put out surveys
   d. Fire people who don't agree
   e. Put in change machines
4. Which of the following are part of the change process?
   a. Helping people see that change is necessary
   b. Helping people see the advantages of change
   c. Helping people recognize that they can make change happen
   d. Getting people fired up and moving forward
   e. All of the above
5. Preparing people for change includes
   a. Providing appropriate training and practice
   b. Training people in groups, not individually, whenever possible
   c. Having leaders and team members training together
   d. Providing space for experimentation and errors
   e. All of the above

10

PROBLEM SOLVING

T he way a business goes about solving a small problem says a lot about how it goes about solving larger, more significant problems. How it views the world and approaches problems is strongly influenced by cultural habits and beliefs. With a small problem, it's easy to see the results of that belief in action because the entire event can be seen at one time; with larger problems, cause and effect may be separated by weeks or months, and the process is often so big that no one ever views it as a whole. The company ends up wondering why its results are poor but can't figure out the reasons. Those small problems can provide valuable insights into the company's methodology and assumptions; recognizing consistent causes of small problems can enable you to avoid large ones. Ultimately, more important than improving the solution to one problem is improving how the company solves problems in general.

WHAT IS THE PROBLEM WITH PROBLEMS?

A commonality between college students and businesspeople is the disturbingly frequent tendency to solve the wrong problems or answer the wrong questions. A solution is only useful if it solves the actual problem. Solving the wrong problem can be expensive in time, resources, and enthusiasm. Effective problem solving involves being able to correctly identify the problem and having a mechanism for generating, testing, and implementing solutions. It's also important to be able to make decisions along the way; indeed, without effective decision-making skills, problem solving becomes virtually impossible, to say nothing of functional leadership, team building, hiring, or motivation.

Chrome

The first step in solving a problem is identifying whether you're dealing with the problem, the symptoms, or the chrome. Chrome is, essentially, those random glittery factors that appear to be associated with the problem but really have little or nothing to do with it. A famous example of chrome is the response to Richard Reid, the infamous "shoe bomber."

Reid attempted to blow up an airplane by igniting an explosive in his shoes. Of course, lighting one's shoes on fire is a bit conspicuous, especially on a no-smoking flight, and he was quickly subdued. The response to Mr. Reid is that we must all take off our shoes and put them through the security scanner at the airport. We should be duly grateful that the 2009 "Christmas bomber," who attempted to ignite his "Fruit of the Boom" underwear aboard a plane, didn't lead to a requirement that we all wear our underwear on the outside.

This is chrome. It is grabbing hold of some superficial aspect of the problem that we think we can control and becoming fixated on it. Dealing with chrome not only wastes time and energy, it can also undermine credibility and faith in the ability of the organization to actually deal with the problem. Dealing with chrome is extremely attractive because it makes us feel like we're doing something. We are Taking Action. We are Responding to the Situation. We are Being Decisive. We are Running Out of Platitudes.

Dealing with chrome follows a pattern similar to Shrinks-R-Us and their organizational OCD. The initial problem causes fear, anger, and other negative emotions. The organization responds by dealing with some aspect of the situation. The very fact of taking action relieves the stress, and everyone starts to feel better. Unfortunately, since only the chrome has been removed, the problem swiftly returns. Now the stress is worse because everyone thought the problem solved. The organization responds by going after more chrome, and so it goes.

Therefore, the first step in effective problem solving is ignoring the chrome. The second step is identifying the problem.

How Long Has That Hurt?

When you visit the doctor, you describe the complaint. The doctor then asks questions, which may or may not seem related to the initial complaint: "I'm here because my throat hurts! Why are you asking me if I'm experiencing shortness of breath?"

The doctor, of course, is inquiring about your symptoms. You've come in with a problem, and she's making sure that your symptoms are consistent with the problem you've described. If they're not, the doctor wants to know about it. She doesn't want to make the wrong diagnosis, or treat the symptoms instead of the disease.

Similarly, workplace problems first present as symptoms. Those symptoms will hopefully lead you to recognize the problem, but they are not the problem. The symptoms are, and always will be, the symptoms. It's important to identify the symptoms and then as many manifestations of those symptoms as possible. Not all symptoms will manifest in all situations.

For example, at Robotic Chromosomes, there appeared to be several "problems": First, documentation was frequently not matched to the actual shipping software. Second, customer support was frequently unable to help clients use certain features of the program. Third, marketing was complaining that demos were failing in very embarrassing ways.

These were all symptoms of the real problem. The actual problem was that there was no overarching design or schedule of releases. No one knew what was in each release, so documentation couldn't figure out what to write, customer support didn't realize that users were trying to use features that didn't exist, marketing was trying to demonstrate features that they'd asked for but no one had actually implemented, and so on. The solution was to create actual schedules with actual lists of features so that everyone involved knew what was going to be in each release. Each department had to learn to talk, and listen, to the others.

Once you've identified the symptoms, the next step is to start brainstorming possible causes. Sometimes the problem will be obvious; other times it may not be. You may come up with one possibility, or with several. In the latter case, you need to go through each possibility and try to determine if it appears to produce the observed symptoms. There's no magic formula for doing this; you just have to work through it. Like anything else, it gets easier with practice.

Once you have a possible problem identified, see if you can break it down. Identify what you can change and what you can't. For example, you probably can't change the economy, but you can change how you deal with it. Tom Watson used the Great Depression as an opportunity to build up a highly trained, extremely loyal workforce and a stockpile of equipment.

When World War II started, IBM was in an excellent position to capitalize on the reawakening economy. If everything falls into the "can't change" category, revisit your problem formulation.

Take This and Call Me in the Morning

Now that you have a working problem formulation, the next step is to generate possible solutions. Once again, you need to brainstorm. Record ideas and do not evaluate any of them until you have a significant number of possibilities. Don't worry if some ideas are silly or off-the-wall. Innovative solutions come from the most unlikely sources. Your goal is to come up with a number of different possibilities. Frequently the silly or off-the-wall idea that's presented early becomes the nugget of the solution later.

Here's an important caveat on brainstorming: any brainstorming session, to be effective, needs people to be creative and invested in solving the problem. Therefore, avoid sessions that go all day. People will get tired, bored, and frustrated, and eventually will become unable to focus or contribute useful ideas. Pushing only generates bad ideas. Brainstorming requires breaks for food or a walk to let your creative juices recharge. It also helps to conduct brainstorming in an environment that is conducive to creative thought. Monochromatic windowless conference rooms do not qualify. Most people are much more creative in spaces where there is natural lighting and color. Since creativity can't be forced, create the conditions to make it likely.

Once you think you have a solution, it's not yet time to implement it. You need to do some more homework. You need to figure out if the solution you've chosen will actually solve your problem. This requires taking some time to forecast the consequences of implementing your solution and determining if it'll get you where you think it will.

Ed Schein points out that when it comes to evaluating solutions, the two most popular methods are expert opinions and previous experience. Unfortunately, neither is always, or even particularly, reliable. It is far better to look for some examples of your solution in practice, perhaps in other organizations that have implemented something similar, and see if you can learn anything from that, or conduct your own tests and research. The latter two approaches are more time-consuming and difficult, but they are also more likely to yield useful data. Using multiple methods of evaluation is also advisable: if you get different results, you have a clue that you might be overlooking something or that one of your methods is invalid. When you use at least two methods, you're more likely to catch errors early.

I've occasionally sat in meetings where someone present will decry the idea of looking at how another organization solved a similar problem as being somehow disloyal. This attitude is parochial at best, flat out disastrous at worst. It's always better to learn from someone else's mistakes whenever possible. You do, however, have to do sufficient homework to make sure that the similarities between your organization and the other organization are not so superficial as to make the comparison worthless.

Once you've developed at least one potential solution, you can finally look at taking action.

Ready, Fire, Aim

Just because it's now possible to take action doesn't mean that you're actually ready to. Before you can start, you need to figure out what it is you're doing.

The first step is clearly defining the team's outcome goal: what will the world look like when the team implements its solution? As you define the goal and specify the details, it's worth taking a moment to make sure that you still believe the solution you're implementing will actually get you there. Remember that part of defining the goal includes specifying a target deadline. The more people who are involved, the more important this is.

If you discover that your solution and goal don't match, you need to redefine the goal or reevaluate your potential solution.

Once the goal is defined, you need to make sure you'll know whether or not you've accomplished it. In other words, you should start defining your criteria for success before you've even started implementing your solution. If you leave the criteria until you're deep into the process of accomplishing the goal, it's much harder to develop unbiased standards, and the process is likely to devolve into pointless argument. The more time and energy you put into something, the more pressure there is to believe that you're doing the right thing. This is particularly true with groups.

Once you've defined your ultimate outcome goal and your standards of evaluation, then it's time to decompose your goal. You need to define your process goals, learning goals, and intermediate outcome goals and figure out how they will be implemented by each member of the team. These are your action steps.

It is usually easier to define your goals through reverse goal-chaining, working backward from your final goal rather than forward from where you are now. That helps build motivation and commitment as part of the planning process.

Remember to define your standards of evaluation for your intermediate goals. It's important to know if the team is on track or not. Naturally, it may not always be possible to define everything at the beginning. That's fine; just remember to include a goal to review and refine future goals and checkpoints. If you find that you can't define intermediate goals or there's no way to evaluate progress, you may need to reevaluate either your goals or the solution you're trying to implement.

As you define your goals, you'll be able to start taking action. Remember to designate times for people to report back to the group about progress. Goals are not worth much if you have no one keeping track of them.

When the team has finally accomplished all its goals and achieved its overall outcome goal, there's still one step left: evaluating success. According to the metrics that you started with, did you actually implement the solution to the problem? Did the problem go away?

Sometimes, despite your best efforts, you will get to the end and discover that the problem formulation was incorrect and you've just solved the wrong problem. If that happens, you'll have to start again with the problem formulation. However, how you frame the experience matters a great deal.

You can view the entire exercise as a waste of time and resources, as a major screwup, and feel extremely discouraged. Or, you can recognize that while you didn't fix the problem you had set out to fix, you still managed to create ancillary benefits and celebrate those successes. For example, you might have significantly improved how well the members of the team work together. The second way of framing the result will leave you, and your team, more energized to try again.

MAKE A DECISION!

The board of directors of a certain organization needed to make a decision on a controversial issue. After days of debate, they held a vote. As soon as the results were announced, the screaming began: "the options weren't clearly explained," "I thought this meant something else," "I assumed that . . . ," and so forth. The debate after the vote was more, shall we say, "intense" than the debate leading up to the vote.

In the end, the board annulled the vote.

This was, perhaps, not the best possible way to make a decision.

Poor decision making interferes with effective problem solving. The problem-solving techniques that we've discussed in this chapter will not function if your organization cannot effectively make and carry out decisions. Therefore, it's worth spending the time to develop good decision-making skills.

Decision-making ability is partially a function of group development. Certain types of decision making work better in some situations, and some methods don't work at all in others. Ed Schein discusses six different types of decision making, which we will explore in the following sections.

The Plop Method

We'll start with the most popular method of decision making. In the "plop" method, an idea is brought up. Before anyone can respond, another idea is tossed out for consideration, causing the first idea to plop to the floor where it sits until someone steps in it. The process continues, and the plops rain down until the group latches on to an idea that it likes.

The problem is that ideas are evaluated only by how long it takes before someone else can come up with another idea. Ideas proposed early in the process are more likely to be lost than ideas proposed later, if only because people start slowing down when they get tired. An idea is as likely to be accepted as a way to end a frustrating meeting as for any inherent value of the idea.

The fundamental assumption underlying the plop method is that silence means a lack of agreement. At a deeper level, the plop method reflects uncertainty about the goals, how to evaluate progress, and an understanding of group capability. Functionally, the plop method is most likely to occur in the Forming and Storming stages. Indeed, if you observe the plop method in a group that's been in existence for months or years, you can safely bet that group is stuck in one of those stages. The plop method is symptomatic of a lack of caring on the part of the team, which generally equates to limited team development. People let ideas plop to the floor because they aren't sufficiently invested in any of the possible solutions or potential outcomes.

I'm in Charge Here!

In any group there is typically someone endowed with legitimate power. Frequently, that person will also be the decider. The decider may choose to collect input from the group, or she may simply gather the information herself and then make a decision.

This sort of decision by formal authority, or autocratic rule, is particularly common in Forming. It may happen in Storming, although there is more likely to be pushback. Groups do not typically make it to Norming or Performing if they have an autocratic decision-making structure. While efficient, a dictatorship does not take full advantage of the hands, eyes, and brains of the team.

When all decisions are made by one person, the assumption is that that person is more capable of making decisions than the group. That's true when the problems are sufficiently easy. However, it becomes steadily less likely as the complexity of the situation increases.

When there is only one person making decisions, the team is wasting other resources within the team itself.

Nonetheless, when a team is in Forming, it's often hard to use any other form of decision making. Team members are still sufficiently uncertain about their goals and their places in the team to be able to meaningfully participate in a more democratic style of leadership. It's important for leaders to recognize that autocracy is a tool with a limited life span and that maintaining it will cap productivity. Remember that personal power is increased when you can give up the use of legitimate, reward, and coercive powers. In this case, building your team to where it can become more democratic may decrease your autocratic, or legitimate, power but increases your referent power and influence and creates a more effective team.

Minority Report

As ludicrous as it may sound, sometimes a group bases all its decisions on the rule of the minority. This is, again, most common in early-stage groups in which the lack of effective group communication and structure make it possible for a single person or coalition to hijack the decision-making process.

In minority rule, an idea is proposed, and the person who proposed it immediately follows the idea with something like this: "Any objections? No? Good. Let's move on."

Sometimes, two or more people will form a coalition. One person will propose the idea, and another will quickly move to hijack the discussion.

This frequently ends up benefiting the minority at the expense of the rest of the team and the larger organization.

Minority rule occurs most often when the members of the team each assume that everyone else knows more than they do and thus are unwilling to speak up. The greater the goal clarity and the higher the affiliation and competence in the group, the more likely it is that someone will challenge the minority and begin a discussion of the idea proposed.

Minority rule can also occur when everyone assumes that they know what the other people are thinking and there is a high degree of conformity in the group: affiliation is too great and/or autonomy is too low. In this case, someone may propose an idea, and everyone goes along with it because they assume that's what the group wants. Again, this reluctance to rock the boat is common in both Forming and Storming. It can sometimes occur in Norming, especially if Storming was particularly nasty.

Minority rule can also occur in conditions of extreme competition, when the minority is more concerned with gaining power, or at least making the majority look bad.

No matter the reason for minority rule, it's important to stop it as soon as you realize it's going on. Minority rule implicitly compromises the autonomy and competence of the rest of the team. It's important to slow things down and make sure that the entire team is comfortable with the idea and actually understands the implications. If you do nothing, you can easily end up with rule by prima donna.

And the Winner Is . . .

We now come to a popular and familiar method of decision making: voting. Voting has the primary advantage that it is culturally normative for most people living in Western democracies. Despite this, it is not necessarily the best method for actually making decisions.

The problem with voting is that losing a vote doesn't necessarily convince the losing side that they are wrong. Rather, it can convince them that they just didn't do a good enough job of persuading the group to vote their way. In some cases, even the spectacular failure of the ideas themselves is not seen as a reason to repudiate the ideas.

For example, back in the late 1990s, Silicon Valley became enamored with the Japanese concept of the *keiretsu*. Keiretsu are companies with interlocking boards of directors. In theory, keiretsu are supposed to make companies stronger. When Japan's economy crashed, the interlocking companies ended up pulling one another down. It's not entirely clear why Silicon Valley investors loved this idea, but they were widely trumpeting it even as existing keiretsu were collapsing around them. The spectacular failure of the keiretsu was not enough to convince many investors that keiretsu were a bad idea. A vote would have only, at best, masked the problem.

Another problem with voting is that the minority may not even agree that majority rule is an appropriate or valid way of reaching agreement! They may feel that it is being forced on them by the majority. In such a situation, the minority is more likely to become a quiet coalition dedicated to undermining the majority.

Voting works when everyone involved feels that they've had their day in court. When one faction strongly disagrees, the worst thing you can do is shove the decision down their throats. Instead, use negotiation: How can you view things from their perspective and make backing the majority's approach the path of least resistance? How can you gain their cooperation without infringing on their autonomy or their sense of competence, and without damaging their affiliation to the group?

Can We Come to a Consensus Here?

Consensus doesn't mean that everyone agrees. In other words, unanimity is not the goal. Rather, consensus means this:

- Everyone understands the issues.
- Everyone feels they've had their say.
- Everyone feels that they've been listened to.
- Everyone is ready to make a decision.
- Everyone is willing to support the decision made by the group.

There are two ways to determine if everyone in the group has reached consensus. The first, and most common method, is mind reading, which happens when the leader assumes that all of the above conditions are true and moves forward with a vote. Mind reading is fairly difficult and should only be attempted by those who have demonstrated their skill in other venues, for example, by winning a fortune playing poker in Vegas. While you might get away with mind reading in a Forming group, it can quickly turn nasty if the group is in Storming.

For the rest of us, it's far more effective to use the opportunity to build competence and autonomy by periodically polling the group:

- Does everyone here feel that they've had the chance to express their views? If someone says no, invite him to contribute his thoughts.
- Does everyone feel that they have enough information to make a decision? If someone says no, ask her what additional information she needs.
- Does everyone feel that they can support whatever decision the group agrees on? If someone says no, ask him what his reservations are and what would have to change for him to no longer have those reservations.

Only when everyone answers "yes" to all three questions do you conduct your vote. As with all things, the process of developing consensus becomes easier with practice.

Recognize that consensus can be time-consuming and difficult, especially in a Forming or Storming group. You may very well find that you are starting with autocratic leadership and moving to a more consensus-based model. That's OK. Those early-stage groups still have limited ability to communicate effectively and have not yet built up a strong sense of trust. Your job is to help them improve their skills in those areas so that they can engage in more productive and effective decision making.

One of the biggest challenges you face in guiding a team toward consensus is dealing with the person who is convinced that there are two ways of doing everything: his way and the wrong way.

Having someone who refuses to compromise with the group is both a positive and a negative. On the plus side, it forces the group to examine alternatives and consider issues that might have otherwise been ignored. On the minus side, it can turn every meeting into an agonizingly long, frustrating experience that shuts down innovation, problem solving, and brainstorming; destroys productivity; and dooms the team to mediocre levels of performance. The trick is to grab as much of the benefits as possible while minimizing the negatives. This is not necessarily easy!

It's important to avoid making someone lose face, and it's important to provide specific feedback. The first step, therefore, is to meet privately with the employee who is refusing to compromise. Explore his reasons. He might be right! Assuming, though, that this is an issue of choosing between multiple viable options, explain to him what your concerns are, with reference to specific incidents, conversations, and discussions. Explain why you are concerned with his behavior. If that doesn't produce any change in his behavior, meet with him again and ask him what he thinks will happen if his behavior doesn't change. You are now applying the principle of leaving things to his imagination.

Depending on how valuable you consider the employee, if there is still no change, you might set up behavioral goals to help him develop better team-related skills. In the end, though, if he refuses to change, the price of having him on the team will eventually outweigh any benefits you might obtain. If you do have to fire someone because he or she can't work with the team, remember to take the time to review your hiring process and see if there's a way to prevent that from happening in the future.

Can't We All Agree?

The theoretically optimal form of decision making is unanimous consent. In the real world, this is rare and difficult to accomplish. It is rarely going to be worth your time and energy to obtain unanimity—far better to reach a consensus that everyone can work with. High-performance teams are rarely unanimous; rather, they excel at achieving consensus and at enthusiastically working on the solution that the team has agreed to.

WHAT ABOUT THE PEOPLE INVOLVED?

A very important aspect of problem solving is recognizing that your solutions need to be carried out by real people in the real world. More broadly, you can view any process or set of rules in your organization as being "solutions" that people have to be able to work with and live with.

When the Soviet Union tried growing wheat in Siberia, they claimed that growing the wheat in inhospitable climes would cause the wheat to become stronger. I often see businesses take the same attitude with the processes that they design for their employees. It didn't work with the wheat, and it doesn't work a whole lot better with people.

A common refrain is, "Oh, how hard can that be? It'll only take someone five minutes!"

That's probably true, and if you could be sure that you'd have only one of "that," it wouldn't be an issue. However, when you have a dozen of "that," now it's an hour. If you have a hundred, that's a good bit of the day.

Part of designing any solution or implementing any process is to consider how that process will be carried out. That may mean involving the implementers in the design process.

When Is Less More?

A common flaw in many processes is that they attempt to overcontrol the situation. The more control you exert, the less autonomy people perceive themselves as having. When that perception is reinforced through the reward and punishment structure of your company, you will often find that one response is that people will refuse to take any initiative—even when you want them to. Or, they'll assert autonomy in ways that are hard to object to but that are not particularly productive.

You don't want people to have to work hard to follow the rules or execute the processes needed to get work done. The more people have to pay attention to and consciously think about the rules, the less attention and thought they have available for actually doing work. You want to make it as easy as possible for them to do their jobs and be productive. The more they feel like they have to fight the system, the lower your product or service quality will be.

At one company, engineers are so tightly scheduled that every minute of their time is allocated. If someone is fixing a bug and discovers some new problem, that engineer will be punished if she takes the time to deal with that problem. If it's not on the list, it's not to be worked on! As a result, engineers are sneaking into the office late at night or on weekends and holidays to fix the things that management doesn't consider important but which are actively preventing other work from getting done. Too much control is preventing the company from responding in a timely and effective manner to relatively small problems, which eventually become very large problems with sharp teeth. In a very direct sense, the company is strangling autonomy and suffering the consequences of that decision.

Maintaining Autonomy

One of the hardest things about designing workplace policies and procedures is maintaining the autonomy of those who need to follow those policies. This comes back to that illusion of control: the idea that we can maximize performance by maximizing control. This might even work if your organization were composed primarily of robots.

I was recently interviewed about certain companies banning Facebook at work. The general tenor of the article was that Facebook amounts to employees taking time from the company or using company equipment for personal use. My response was a little different and focused around the principles that I've discussed in this chapter and this book. I pointed out that the use of social networking and the ubiquity of smartphones that can access sites such as Facebook mean that employers cannot easily ban social networking. Instead, employers need to become considerably more skilled at clearly defining goals and metrics for evaluation.

That way, it doesn't matter whether employees are on Facebook or not. They know what is expected from them, by when, and how they'll be evaluated. If they don't live up to the standards, the employer can take whatever action is deemed appropriate.

This approach removes the conflict over Facebook, lets the employer treat the employees like adults and not children, and gives the employees the power to make their own choices, preserving autonomy.

Giving people the power to make their own choices means that sometimes they'll make choices that you don't like. If they're accomplishing their goals, supporting the team, and contributing to a positive work environment, this may not be a problem. If it is a problem, much of the time it can be remedied through feedback and training. However, when that fails, you need to understand why. Are they being rewarded for those poor choices? If so, change the incentives. Do those poor choices make sense from their perspective? Find out why so that you can deal with the problem, not the symptom. If all else fails, though, perhaps the correct answer is not to tighten the rules but to recognize that someone who consistently makes poor choices for your organization does not belong there.

Sun, Rise! Sun, Set!

In the classic children's story *The Little Prince*, the King tells the Little Prince that he can command the sun to rise and set, but only at the proper times.

One of the secrets to getting people to comply with office policies is to create policies that they will comply with. That doesn't mean that everyone has to like everything; it does mean that policies need to be perceived as fair. You need to consider how your policies will be implemented and how they will interact with autonomy, affiliation, and competence. When a policy is unpopular and hard to enforce, there is always a tendency to honor it in the breech.

Fundamentally, when policies are routinely ignored, the entire structure of your existing policies is undermined. You are sending a clear message that anything goes as long as you don't get caught or as long as the right people benefit. That attitude cost John Gutfreund control of Salomon Brothers back in the early 1990s. He turned a blind eye to a rogue trader breaking the rules. When the news finally broke, the company was nearly destroyed, and Gutfreund was forced to resign.

You don't have to be an investment bank playing games with the Federal Reserve to run into problems. Even when some policies are honored in the breech, it will rarely be the case that everyone ignores those policies. The people who respect the rules will eventually notice that other people are ignoring them. That can lead to the perception that some people are "special" and that the workplace is unfair. A perception of unfairness will build resentment and internal competition. That, in turn, undermines affiliation and decreases performance. If you're lucky, the problem will eventually bubble up to your attention. If you're unlucky, it'll fester, sapping performance.

Don't make rules that you are unwilling to enforce, and don't be afraid to enforce rules that are on the books for a good reason. Above all, take the time to build policies, rules, and procedures that are unobtrusive and easy to follow. If you are going to exempt some people from certain rules, make sure everyone understands how that comes about. You can do a great deal so long as people perceive that the rules are fair.

WHAT ABOUT ETHICS?

In many ways, ethics is one of the trickiest problems faced by organizations. The topic of ethics is one that often ignites a great deal of controversy in every venue where I've seen it come up. In many cases, such as high-technology companies where I worked or businesses for whom I consult, a discussion of ethics often is equated as a personal attack on members of the organization.

Ethics, in the most common sense, is considered to be that behavior that is morally accepted as "good" and "right." The problem with ethics is that it isn't always that simple. One person's version of what is good and right isn't always the same as another's. Some companies will lay off some employees on the grounds that it's a necessary evil to preserve the jobs of the rest; Tom Watson, the founder of IBM, regarded such behavior as unethical. Despite pressure from investors, he refused to lay off employees even during the Great Depression.

More generally, ethics is a tool to educate the members of an organization and nonmembers alike. Nonmembers are those people who are not employed by an organization or who do not qualify for membership for any of a number of reasons. For example, most of us are nonmembers of the American Medical Association. Members are told the behavioral expectations involved in being part of the organization. This is particularly important in organizations in which there are new members constantly entering the group. Without this education, members unwittingly may act contrary to the norms and desires of the group, or unscrupulous group members may take advantage of the ignorance of younger group members. Because so much of learning ethical behavior in a group involves modeling established members, it is particularly important that those members live up to the principles espoused by the organization and that the organization enforce, visibly when necessary, the appropriate behavior. Ethical behavior, in other words, is comprised of outcome, process, and learning goals: outcome, to achieve certain objective behaviors or avoid certain situations; process, because ethical behavior is ongoing; and learning, because members of the organization need to learn that organization's ethical standards.

Group Standards

Nonmembers, on the other hand, learn what behavior to expect from members of the group. In a sense, the code of ethics of a group can also be considered its list of qualifications. The ethics code of the American Psychological Association (APA) states the expected skills and qualifications of a therapist. By doing so, it educates the public, who are largely nonmembers of the APA, as to what it believes to be the necessary qualifications of a therapist.

When a person sees a purported member of an organization behaving in a way that does not match the stated ethics of an organization, it may be a clue that the person is not, in reality, a member of the organization or is acting without the organization's knowledge or approval. Without the knowledge of what the organization considers ethical, an observer might otherwise condemn the entire organization based on the actions of one or a few individuals.

Ultimately, organizational ethics define the range of accepted and acceptable behaviors within an organization. To be effective, the commitment to live up to them must be made throughout the organization. This, in turn, requires that ethical considerations be built into organizational culture, processes, and goals. If not, the very act of setting a goal may preclude consideration of the ethical issues around it.

How Do We Get Ethical Behavior?

You get what you demonstrate, pay attention to, and reward. If you want ethical behavior in your company, you must do the following:

- Act as a role model for the behavior you want. Define the end point so that people can see what's expected of them.
- Pay attention to the behavior going on around you. When you see unethical behavior, find the reasons and change them. Actively discourage unethical behavior, including firing people if necessary. When a problem comes to your attention, move rapidly. Don't let it fester. Remove causes and temptations whenever possible. Institute policies when needed, but no more than absolutely necessary.
- Reward the behaviors you want to see. Hold them up as examples, and demonstrate that you are paying attention and that you care. Make it easy for people to behave ethically. You're not running a morality play, you're trying to get results.

If you want ethical behavior, make it a goal and make sure that the feedback is there.

Review Quiz

1. In order to effectively solve a problem, you should
   a. Focus exclusively on the chrome
   b. Identify the symptoms and treat them
   c. Identify the symptoms and let them lead you to the problem
   d. Ignore it; it will go away
   e. None of the above
2. The assumption behind the plop method of decision making is that
   a. Silence means lack of agreement
   b. The group knows best
   c. The leader wanted it that way
   d. Everyone is in agreement
   e. All of the above

3. Minority rule is most likely to occur in groups in
   a. Forming and Storming
   b. Storming and Norming
   c. Forming and Performing
   d. Forming, Storming, and Norming
   e. All stages
4. Autocratic rule works best
   a. In early-stage groups
   b. When problems are complex
   c. When problems are simple
   d. a & b
   e. a & c
5. Rules in a company should
   a. Cover all aspects of corporate life
   b. Be ones that you're willing to enforce
   c. Be easy to follow
   d. Be unobtrusive
   e. b, c, & d
6. The keys to generating ethical behavior in your company are
   a. Be a role model
   b. Pay attention to the behaviors going on around you
   c. Reward the behaviors you want to see
   d. Make lots of speeches about ethical behavior
   e. a, b, & c

CHAPTER 11

MISTAKES: THE FOUNDATION OF INNOVATION

I am frequently told that the goal of business is to make money. While making money is a nice thing, it makes a lousy goal. The goal of business is to provide a stream of products and services that people perceive as providing value. Money is how you know you're succeeding. Money is feedback that you are moving toward your goal. It is not the goal.

WHAT IS THE GOAL OF MY BUSINESS?

In sports, an athlete who only sets outcome goals, such as winning the competition, will typically seek less and less challenge and become less willing to experiment and test her skills in more difficult situations. Successful athletes set process goals as well as outcome goals; the process goals keep them focused on the behaviors that make the outcome goals likely.

Developing products and services is a process. Making money is the outcome goal. Since making money is an outcome goal, when money becomes the goal, risk-taking and innovation suffer, just as sports performance suffers in an outcome-oriented athlete. Outcome-oriented athletes are more prone to cheating and more subject to depression when they lose. Similarly, businesses that are focused only on making money tend to engage in counterproductive behaviors, are more likely to violate ethical norms, and are more likely to see the organizational equivalent of depression. Morale collapses, discontent increases, loyalty evaporates, team cohesion and motivation dissolves, internal conflict erupts, and eventually employees flee the company in search of greener pastures.

The world is full of once-innovative companies that were dethroned by upstarts.

Despite their great expertise in retail, Wal-Mart and Barnes & Noble were "Amazon'd" when the Internet came along. Even now, fifteen years after Amazon.com opened its doors, Wal-Mart and B&N are still having trouble competing with it.

Even though they dominated the film industry, both Polaroid and Kodak failed to see digital cameras developing. By the time they embraced the new technology, it was too little, too late.

After getting a small push from Microsoft, IBM fell out a Window. IBM dominated the computer industry and even created the IBM PC. IBM's own creation created Microsoft and Dell, which proceeded to thrash Big Blue in, respectively, the operating system and PC markets.

Microsoft, in its turn, is becoming increasingly less relevant as Google's star waxes stronger. Dick Brass, a former Microsoft VP, wrote recently in the *New York Times* that although Microsoft's past is wonderful, its future is less clear. Microsoft's much vaunted Bing search engine hasn't dented Google's dominance of the search market.

In each of these companies, the organizational culture that made the business successful paralyzed it at a critical moment. In each case, the organization went from bold and risk-taking to timid. Of course, they didn't call it timid. They used other words, like *stability* or *measured investment*, or *careful progress*, or whatever. In short, though, they were not willing to make mistakes.

MAKE MORE MISTAKES

To get past the basics and actually develop a deeper understanding of any art or skill, one has to be willing to make a lot of mistakes. When I speak on creativity and innovation, what upsets people the most is the recommendation that they need to make more mistakes. Quite simply, companies that tolerate flashy, expensive mistakes are also the companies that are most likely to come up with the successful, unusual products. Big success requires a willingness to fail.

Back in the 1990s, Apple came out with a PDA called the Apple Newton. It was a miserable flop. Many people were busy writing Apple off, assuming that was the end of the company. Today, the iPod Touch and the iPhone are ubiquitous.

Being willing to make a mistake worked out pretty well in the end.

We are taught in school that we must avoid mistakes. Mistakes mean a lower grade and potential failure. In business, mistakes cost money, and wasting money is a cardinal sin. Mistakes are *bad*. If nothing is learned from losing money on a mistake, only then is it a waste. Making the same mistake over and over again, now that's a problem!

The Efficiency Paradox

One of the big problems with mistakes is that we view them as inefficient. An efficient system is frequently described as one in which there are no mistakes.

People, however, only learn by making mistakes.

This creates a bit of a problem. In a truly efficient system, there would be no opportunity for people to learn. When there is no learning, the system will eventually fail. Either it becomes rigid or it stagnates, but in either case it fails to adapt to changing conditions in the environment. Innovation decreases as intolerance for mistakes increases. Cultures are the residue of success, of lessons learned over time. Learning those lessons is comforting, and knowing how not to get burned a second time is generally a good thing. Unfortunately, innovation only comes about when you're willing to risk that burn.

Now, there are certainly situations in which there is no room for mistakes—surgery and landing an airplane are two that come to mind. However, in order for someone to become a master surgeon or a successful pilot, he or she had to make a lot of mistakes along the way. The goal, of course, is to make sure those mistakes occur in settings that do not involve people getting killed. And, although both of these professionals are required to perform potentially difficult operations without error, they are also expected to rapidly recognize and adjust to changing circumstances, for example, having both engines of your airplane taken out of action by birds. That ability to adjust can only come from experience in dealing with unexpected or unusual situations, in other words, coping with mistakes without losing your mental balance.

I've seen CEOs comfortably running their companies, apparently supremely confident, right up until something unexpected happens: revenue misses expectations, there's an unforeseen problem with the product, a deadline has to be extended, or a similar setback occurs. The response is pure panic. In one case, the CEO simply refused to acknowledge the unexpected problem and insisted on shipping on schedule anyway—and then couldn't understand why the customers were so irate. In another situation, the first time revenue came in light, the CEO immediately laid off 20 percent of the company. This was not a particularly well-considered response to the situation. In both of these scenarios, the CEO didn't stop to think; instead, he took the fact that Something Was Wrong, imagined the most dire of consequences, and simply acted.

The problem with innovation is that it's a process that feels inefficient and requires a great willingness to make mistakes. When a company is first starting out, it's easy to innovate because it's that or die. As the company evolves, though, innovation can become more difficult or focus more and more on improving products and processes with which the company is already comfortable. Mistakes are more and more often seen as punishable offenses rather than opportunities to create the next big thing. The fear of mistakes starts to prevent experimentation and exploration. Tolerance for risk gradually decreases as the company becomes convinced that it is in control of its environment. The goal is to make the right mistakes!

WHAT IS THE CONNECTION BETWEEN ORGANIZATIONAL CULTURE AND INNOVATION?

A company is never truly in control of its environment. However, a company with a strong track record of success and that has developed a strong corporate culture may come to believe that it controls its environment. IBM in the 1980s, for example, dominated the computer industry. This domination led to a belief that it controlled the environment; its domination would continue indefinitely. Instead, the environment changed. It turned out that what IBM truly dominated was the mainframe market, and the company was caught flat-footed by the success of its own product, the PC.

On a cultural level, IBM had learned the lessons of its own success far too well. It was so used to its name and reputation being enough to sell products that it was not prepared to deal with the individual market, where IBM's name and reputation did not have the same cachet.

On a broader level, IBM was a victim of its own successes. It had learned the lessons of how to sell big iron, and those lessons became part of the corporate culture. They became automatized behaviors. IBM reflexively applied those lessons to a new market and a new breed of engineers and ended up in deep trouble. Eventually, in 1992, IBM imploded. What saved the company, beyond bringing in Lou Gerstner, was that the crisis also reactivated IBM's innovative streak. Faced with destruction, the company was willing to take risks again. It took a big hit at the time but came back strong.

By contrast, GM was also having financial problems in the late 1980s and early 1990s. It, too, had learned significant lessons about success over the course of its history. GM was one of the original automakers and, like IBM, a survivor of the Great Depression. GM also acted according to the lessons of its history and culture. Rather than recognize that it had less control of its environment than it thought, GM withdrew from markets it didn't think it could dominate and focused more and more on advertising campaigns instead of building high-quality cars. Its innovations were entirely in the area of advertising and fiddling with the little details. GM was not, however, building the types of cars that Americans wanted to buy. The net result was that in the Great Recession of 2008–2009, GM went bankrupt and had to be rescued by the government. Once a brilliant, innovative company, it had become a symbol of incompetence. Avoidance is not a good strategy for coping with anxiety at either the individual or the organizational level.

The Problem with "Radical" Innovation

Radical innovation is a scary concept for most people. It requires moving outside the safe territory established by organizational culture in its function as an anxiety-reducing agent and in its encoding of the memes that tell people how to respond to environmental changes and challenges. To the extent that culture encodes lessons that lead to success, innovations that extend existing products and methods of doing things are often seen as more congruent with cultural mores than radical innovations, which often attack the accepted way things are done or lead to significant cultural change.

Radical innovations, almost by definition, involve leaping boldly forth into unknown territory. Success is impossible to predict, and precise costs are difficult to determine. Indeed, progress forward may require a great deal of faith, especially in the early stages. As you'll recall, the executive subculture is concerned with dealing with stockholders and investors. Thus, moving forward with no other justification than faith can be extremely difficult to sell to the executive subculture, which ultimately decides how to allocate resources.

One of the aspects of organizational culture is that it defines the way people are supposed to think. People who think and act too differently may well be excluded from the organization. However, productive argument and constant questioning is vital in successful team innovation. Minority dissent can be quite valuable to innovation when that dissent forces the closer examination of ideas and questioning of assumptions that would otherwise be taken for granted. Thus, innovative behavior and thought walk a fine line between thinking differently but not too differently. This tends to lead to minor innovations, improving the current products or methods of doing things, but not changing them radically. Too radical a level of dissent will frequently result in a crushing response instead of an effort to understand the minority's opinion. Without that attempt at understanding, the value of minority dissent in innovation is lost.

Furthermore, the dissenting minority is not necessarily rewarded for that dissenting voice. Indeed, quite frequently minority dissenters encounter pressure to be more cooperative with the majority. In working with a variety of high-tech companies, my personal observation is that dissent is rarely rewarded, even when it later leads to significant benefits to the organization.

What this boils down to is that, depending on the nature of the specific organization's culture, new ideas will certainly encounter some degree of social resistance, largely proportional to how radical those ideas are and how large a perceived cost there is. To the extent that this resistance translates into a refutation of or disbelief in the innovative ideas, pressure to conform may lead the originator of the idea to become convinced that the idea was wrong to begin with. Indeed, the idea may not even be mentioned if the originator strongly believes that the social pressure against it will be too strong.

We thus see that organizations can be caught up in the pressures of their own success, leading to an organization falling into one or more of several culture traps that can impede or completely stifle innovation.

WHAT ARE THE TRAPS THAT ORGANIZATIONS FALL INTO?

There's a funny thing about innovation: despite all the stories about two guys in a garage, innovation is not the province of the lone genius sitting in a basement somewhere. Or, to put this slightly differently, two guys in a garage can start a company, but they aren't enough to sustain it.

Whenever I speak on innovation, someone always asks me how his company can identify the one or two really creative people. The answer is simple: they're usually the ones you didn't hire or the ones who left to start their own company because they found your company stifling.

Creativity is not the province of one or two people. It is the province of everyone. Innovation is a group effect. It's up to you to create an environment that fosters creativity and innovation. The first step to doing that is avoiding the traps.

The Perfection Trap

Some years ago, I worked for a software start-up that wanted to ship an absolutely perfect version 1.0 product. Of course, no one knew precisely what a perfect product looked like. There was a great deal of very imaginative thinking, but little actual reality was allowed to intrude. Even the customers didn't really know what a perfect product looked like. Without having something to play with, their image changed with the situation.

The result was a moving target: constant feature creep, delays, endless arguments over what was a bug and what was a feature, and so forth. While the product did ship eventually, it did so at the cost of leaving the team exhausted and burned out.

Microsoft, on the other hand, was famous in the 1990s for shipping "beta" software. It correctly deduced that people would rather have usable software now rather than perfect software later. While this was frustrating to some, and downright infuriating to many engineers, as a marketing strategy it worked very well. IBM, it should be noted, did much the same thing in the 1960s and 1970s. In both cases, the companies shipped an "imperfect" product and thereby gave the customers something to play with. The feedback they obtained enabled IBM and Microsoft to further fine-tune their offerings.

This tells us that *good enough* beats perfection. What is good enough? Whatever the customer thinks is good enough. How do you find that out?

You ask, in much the same way as Microsoft and IBM once knew how to ask. That way you don't have to guess.

Naturally, once something is successful, we want to improve on that success. On one level, this is great; the first crude PCs become the elegant laptops that we carry around with us. The first crude iPod becomes the iPod Touch and the iPhone. Each successive improvement is smaller, though. The gap between the first iPhone and the iPhone 3G is much greater than between the 3G and the 3GS. More and more effort is going into perfecting what is already there.

Recall, from our discussions of culture, that whatever is perceived to lead to success is likely to be remembered and become part of the culture. What is usually remembered is not the early, risk-taking behavior. Rather, it is the much more recent and longer process of perfecting the product. The risk itself starts to be forgotten, dismissed as unnecessary, or viewed as incidental to success. The company becomes used to success and forgets how to explore.

As one senior-level partner in a certain firm said to me, "Once I have a sure thing, I stick with it. I don't take risks."

This is the perfection trap in action, the belief that there is no longer a need to take risks. The path to success is to stop taking risks and just perfect what we've got. When a company thinks it knows just what the customer wants, that's the first warning sign of the perfection trap. IBM fell into that trap in the 1980s, and Microsoft is there today.

The Walt Disney Company was originally famed for its cartoons and movies. When it came to theme parks, Walt Disney had to fight tooth and nail with his board to get them to agree to create Disneyland. They saw it as too big a risk. He had the same fight again over Walt Disney World.

Over time, Disneyland and Disney World have only gotten better and better. The problem with the perfect mousetrap is that eventually someone shows up with a cat.

The Protection Trap

Let's move now from the perfection trap to the closely related protection trap, also known as "Don't hurt our existing products!" Perfection and protection are often found together, in large part because the former is frequently a trigger for the latter.

Cisco Systems CEO John Chambers once famously said that Cisco would "eat its own young" before anyone else could. Mr. Chambers had the right idea, and Cisco is one company that's been reasonably successful in sticking to its diet. For the most part, it turns out that eating your own young is easy to say but hard to do.

As we discussed, Kodak and Polaroid were both slow to adopt digital photography, in large part because of their extensive investment in the film business. Nikon, on the other hand, made cameras. They didn't much care what the "film" was, so they had no problem impacting their existing product line. Digital photography was, metaphorically, just another type of film to them.

Let's go back to organizational culture. The products that are making us successful tend to be enshrined in the culture. They are part of how the company works, part of how the company grew, part of how it survives. The company develops a certain loyalty to the product line. Any given product line is, however, not a marriage of love but one of convenience. Competing with existing products by offering a new, revolutionary one can often be seen as disloyal to the company, or at least contrary to the company's beliefs. Furthermore, the more time, energy, and money that have been invested in a product, the harder it is to say good-bye.

By the same token, it's easy to view competing with your own products as "losing," or admitting that you've made a mistake.

The science fiction writer E. E. "Doc" Smith once famously wrote that "what science can synthesize, science can duplicate." If you can come up with ways to compete with your own products, so can someone else. Competitors won't have any compunction, so neither should you. At least if you come out with the better product, you keep the business. The only mistake lies in not responding to the feedback in front of you. Sooner or later, someone will find a way to make hamburger of your cash cow. Just ask the record companies about iTunes, or those bricks-and-mortar bookstores about Amazon.com.

In the end, the protection trap is the belief that if you don't compete with your own products, neither will anyone else. If you believe that, I've got a bridge to sell you. . . .

The Identity Trap

The identity trap occurs when a company says, "We're an X, not a Y."

Around twenty years ago, I proposed developing an AI-based training game at IBM. I was told in no uncertain terms that IBM was a serious manufacturer of business solutions, not a game company. Today, of course, serious games are all the rage, and IBM is a major player.

When a company becomes focused on perfecting its products and starts putting more and more effort into protecting its product line from itself, it risks falling into the identity trap: it starts to define itself as its products. The successes the company has experienced become the definition of the company. Thus, IBM, before it reinvented itself, was a "hardware/mainframe" company. GM is a car company. Walt Disney had to fight with his board to convince them to build theme parks; they saw the organization as a "movie company," and moving into theme parks required a shift in how the company viewed itself.

The identity trap is not entirely a function of the company. Customers, the media, and other outside forces will label the company. Whether or not the company believes the label is a separate issue!

Amazon.com has so far managed to avoid the identity trap. Although it was originally labeled an "online bookstore," it has clearly moved well beyond that. Indeed, Amazon.com has found innovative ways of selling more and more stuff, from DVDs and electronics to the Kindle to cloud computing services.

Apple Computer successfully escaped the identity trap when it changed its name to Apple. Although that name change may appear to be a trivial thing, it reflects a fundamental shift in how the company sees itself. Although Apple still makes computers, they are no longer a computer maker.

The biggest danger of the identity trap is that brainstorming is stifled and ideas are stillborn because no one can see how they fit into the company's identity box.

The Creeping Box Trap

It's a great thing to think outside the box. Indeed, the farther out you can get and still create a viable business, the better. Yahoo in the 1990s was one of the pioneers of Internet search and advertising. Yahoo was offering search at a time when many people didn't see the point. After all, they could keep track of all the websites in their heads. Yahoo's stock performance during the 1990s says something about how far outside the box they were. It was one of the best performing stocks from 1996 to 2000. By then, of course, Internet search was old hat. Along came Google, and once again we're off to the races. However, Google's stock performance, amazing as it has been, is not yet close to what Yahoo's was. Google was not as far outside the box as Yahoo was.

As for Yahoo, what happened to them? Fundamentally, the box got bigger. At one time outside the box, Yahoo was eventually engulfed by it. Whenever you successfully think outside the box, you demonstrate that there's something out there. The box grows. If you don't keep moving, sooner or later you'll be back in the box.

As I write this, Apple just shipped a new iPhone and recently shipped the iPad. While there is still, even after its release, a lot of debate about the merits of the iPad, it has the potential to be a very clever move by Apple: a tablet computer that will generate a tremendous amount of feedback from consumers. Apple will get to see what works and what doesn't, and make money along the way. Unless the iPad is the Newton on steroids, it's going to morph into something much more attractive. Apple has established a beachhead outside the box and is now figuring out what to do next. By the time this book is published, we'll have a good clue how well the company did, especially if you're reading it on an iPad—or a Kindle instead.

In the creeping box trap, the company becomes so focused on polishing its new box that it forgets how to get outside of it. Even worse, the company has become so used to being outside the original box that it does not recognize that it is in a new box.

Thus, culture becomes a two-edged sword. It can simultaneously be the structure that enables an organization to grow and become dominant, and also a check on the organization's ability to adapt when the environment changes. If not managed properly, the strength the organization derives from its culture can also become its greatest weakness and, in the worst case, the source of the organization's destruction.

So what can be done?

THE ART OF NOT MAKING A LIGHTBULB

Thomas Edison once said that he hadn't failed, he'd learned a thousand ways to not make a lightbulb.

That's easy to say. It's hard to live by.

It's not enough to avoid the four innovation traps. There are also four things you need to do in order to foster a consistently innovative environment. Think of avoiding the traps as not driving off a cliff or into a brick wall. Just because you've successfully avoided those fates doesn't mean you'll get where you're going. You still have to put gas in the car, make sure the tires are inflated, stop to eat, and so on. At the risk of going overboard on the metaphors here, playing a good game of golf requires more than just staying out of the sand traps!

Keep Learning

We've discussed the importance of training; giving people the opportunity to learn and improve their skills also improves motivation, job satisfaction, productivity, and loyalty.

There is another benefit. Increased learning leads to increased innovation. The more information people have, the more likely they are to come up with unexpected connections. Encourage people to take classes in a variety of subjects, not just their areas of professional expertise. You never know what synergies will come out of it. Also encourage people to share what they know, talk about it, brainstorm, and have fun with it.

It's important to look at how your organization views continual education: is it a priority or an afterthought? As a clue, consider this: if people are working fifty, sixty, or more hours per week, they're not going to be very interested in taking classes. They'll be tired and view learning as a chore or another demand on their time. If people are spending all their time fighting fires and are subjected to frequent interruptions during the day, they won't be in a mental space to focus on learning. If you want learning to be a priority, you need to fit it into the normal workday. It needs to be viewed as an important part of the job, just as important as anything else people are doing.

Remember, it's not enough to tell people to "be creative." They need to have something to be creative with. The more they know, the better the odds are that they'll come up with something.

Spot Problems Early

I opened the chapter by discussing mistakes. Making mistakes is an integral part of innovation. Innovation is often likened to Athena springing forth fully formed from the brow of Zeus. It is, in a somewhat ironic way, appropriate that a mythological belief should have a mythological reference. Most innovations involve learning a thousand ways to not make the lightbulb before you start to see success. The goal is not perfection, which is not possible, but being the best game in town.

The key to successful innovation is being willing to be wrong a lot of the time. The secret is to be wrong in useful ways. So long as your innovative new product is useful, people will forgive a lot. So long as they like it, they'll give you lots of feedback about how you can improve it. In their heydays, both IBM and Microsoft made good use of that strategy.

Walt Disney is famous for his cartoons and for the movies he made. If you visit Disney World, you can find a video of Walt Disney talking about his thoughts on creating Disney and the Disney theme parks. One of the interesting things he says is that he always wanted to have multiple movies in production at once: he knew that half of them would flop, but he never knew which half. The goal was to make big money on the successful movies and minimize the losses on the flops.

Not all your ideas will work. Not all innovations succeed. The goal is to recognize the mistakes quickly, learn from them, and move on: analyze, evaluate, adjust, not judge and punish. It doesn't take that many successes for a company to do very well indeed, whereas failures are usually only fatal when you refuse to cut your losses and learn from the experience. Both the Apple Newton and the IBM Micro Channel were big, public, expensive flops. So what? Despite the predictions of doom at the time, both companies are doing quite well today. Part of setting effective goals is learning to spot problems early and recognizing how you'll know whether or not you're on track. When you're making the same mistakes over and over, then you have a problem.

However, there is a right way to be wrong!

Take a Break!

While giving a talk one time, I referred to the original "Eureka!" moment: the possibly apocryphal story of Archimedes stepping into the public baths and realizing from the displacement of the water the solution to a problem he was working on. The audience looked at me blankly. It only took a couple of questions to determine that they didn't know who Archimedes was and also didn't know what a eureka moment is. Quite simply, it is that instant when you realize that the solution to a problem you've been working on is staring you in the face and you hadn't seen it. It's a sudden flash of insight. It is said that Archimedes was so excited by his realization that he ran back to his workshop without even bothering to grab his clothes.

That certainly sounds pretty good, if you can get it to happen. Fortunately, there are some easy ways to do that. Unfortunately, there are also ways to make sure that it doesn't happen. Those are even easier.

The easiest way to prevent a eureka moment from occurring is to refuse to take a break. Archimedes had his moment when he put down the problem of figuring out if a crown were made of pure gold and took a break. I've known countless engineers, managers, authors, and so on who all reported solving a difficult problem after walking away from it for a while. Despite that, in company after company, I see people being yelled at for not working hard enough when they solve a problem by walking away from their desks instead of sitting there banging their heads against the proverbial wall. Of course, if a manager has never heard of a eureka moment, it's entirely possible that he doesn't even recognize the possibility that something worthwhile is going on.

Does it make more sense to solve a problem by leaving the office for a couple of hours or to spend eight or ten hours banging your head against the wall and not come up with a solution? Despite this, at one company I heard a manager tell an employee that he "owed the company time" because he didn't solve the problem while sitting at this desk. At another large company, I witnessed a manager tell an employee that he wouldn't be getting a raise because he hadn't solved the problems in the office. This, despite the fact that the employee had finished everything ahead of schedule! In both of these situations, the employee had managed to capture that eureka moment and in both situations was penalized for it.

From the manager's point of view, the employee wasn't working. He might have been walking around the complex or going for a run or at the gym. In one case, she was sitting in another part of the office complex, apparently staring into space. Clearly, people are working only when they look like they're working, right? Well, in jujitsu, the most skilled practitioners look like they aren't doing anything at all as their partners fall down. In fact, I've frequently heard people claiming that the technique was clearly staged, at least until they got thrown. Appearances can often be deceiving.

Taking breaks reduces burnout and increases motivation. It also helps with innovation. As Harvard professor and physician Herbert Benson discusses in depth in *The Breakout Principle*, creative breakthroughs come not when we're pounding our heads against the wall but after we take a break and do something completely different.

That break may be short or long. It may involve walking down the hall to get a cup of coffee or a trip to the gym or listening to music. Some type of physical exercise is often one of the best ways of generating a eureka moment, as exercise dramatically improves concentration and focus. How much of a difference does exercise make? One school found that student behavior, test scores, and concentration all improved dramatically by giving the kids more time to run around. Adults aren't so different. We work best when we mix intense concentration with variety and relaxation. Fortunately, despite Archimedes, it's not necessary to run naked through the streets.

Be Patient

While it's true that too much patience goes nowhere, it is also true that a little patience goes a long way.

For all that necessity is the mother of invention, birth still takes time. There are some things you cannot rush. As the old joke goes, just because a woman can give birth to a baby in nine months, that doesn't mean that nine women can have a baby in one month.

In more prosaic terms, if you wait until your sales are drying up or your competitors are eating your lunch, it's too late. In a perfect world, the time to start building an innovative workforce and organizational culture is on day one. You need to be investing in innovation at exactly the point in time when it seems like you don't need it: when your products are flying high and your stock is going to the moon.

From a practical perspective, that's exactly when you have the most resources, the most enthusiasm, and the most time to take risks. If you wait until the handwriting is on the wall, it's much, much more difficult. Not only are people running scared and your competitors nipping at your heels, you're now in a race against the clock. It's much harder to explore and make mistakes when every mistake feels like it's moving you closer to organizational doom.

IT'S A PROCESS!

Innovation is not a bolt of lightning out of the blue. It's a process. If you wait for the lightning bolt, you're gambling. Viewing innovation as a process gives you control of the situation, or at least lets you put up lightning rods. The process goals and learning goals that you set are critical to shaping an innovative organizational culture or a culture that is constantly playing catch-up. How you regard innovation and crazy ideas will tell people whether you're serious about innovation or just give it lip service. Punish the mistakes that result from exploration and experimentation, and people won't take risks. Reward crazy ideas and you'll get crazy ideas. That's where innovation comes from.

Review Quiz

1. The goal of your business is to
   a. Make money
   b. Reward shareholders
   c. Employ as few people as possible
   d. Create a stream of products and/or services that provide value
   e. All of the above
2. Mistakes
   a. Are highly inefficient and should be eliminated
   b. Must be avoided at all costs
   c. Are a sign of incompetence
   d. Are necessary for innovation and learning
   e. Will destroy any organization
3. Which of the following are cultural innovation traps?
   a. Perfection
   b. Protection
   c. Identity
   d. Creeping box
   e. All of the above
4. Which of the following are necessary steps to increase innovation?
   a. Continuous learning
   b. Making mistakes
   c. Taking breaks
   d. Patience
   e. All of the above

CHAPTER 12

PUTTING IT ALL TOGETHER: SCHEDULING SUCCESS

Time is one of those funny things. No matter how much we talk about saving time, it's never there when we want to make a withdrawal. We can't save it, we can't invest it, we can't put some aside for later use. However, we can approach it in different ways. How we use time can determine the success or failure of a project; the degree of focus and motivation of employees; their ability to concentrate; and even the health of your workforce.

THE ILLUSION OF TIME

Douglas Adams, the author of the popular Hitchhiker's Guide to the Galaxy books, once said that "time is an illusion, lunchtime doubly so."

We measure time using clocks, watches, even our cell phones. These days, it's hard to not know the time. There is a difference, though, between measuring time, experiencing time, and using time. Measuring time is often not particularly useful, and time used well can be very hard to measure! There is a great deal of truth to the old joke that time is simply nature's way of keeping everything from happening all at once (no matter how much we may try!).

Scheduling is the art of managing time so that the appropriate people and resources are always in the right place at the right time. When people are using time effectively and don't feel pressed for time, you know you're on the right track. Since nothing succeeds like the expectation of success, our goal is to schedule success.

Why Not Just Go Faster?

I hear all the time from managers that they come into the office each day with a to-do list. Before they've gotten halfway through it, some crisis hits, and they spend the rest of the day in a blur of motion trying to deal with things as they come up. As a result, they end up exhausted and frustrated, and the to-do list only gets longer.

The action in sports such as fencing or judo is extremely fast. At the same time, paradoxically, speed leads to errors: the faster you go, the more likely you are to miss your target or overcommit to your move, leaving you vulnerable. Experts in these sports appear to be moving at blinding speed, and yet they never seem to rush.

In an office setting, the manager who is forced to spend her day rushing from one crisis to the next is constantly moving at high speed. She has no time to think or plan, only to react. The fencer who is purely reactive loses. You need to get ahead of the other person in order to win. By the same token, you must get ahead of the events in the office in order to be able to make consistently good decisions.

I am frequently told that there just isn't time to stop and think when things are busy. This is an illusion. If you stop and catch your breath for five minutes, you are not going to be stabbed with a sword or slammed into the ground. However, just like the fencer or judoist, the temptation is to move with superhuman speed and solve the problem before the next one arises. This doesn't work all that well. Just as in sports, moving too fast leads to careless errors, limiting our ability to adjust to changing conditions or devise a strategic response to a competitor.

When a team is consistently making careless or sloppy errors, that's a sign that they are going too fast. People who feel rushed don't read instructions as carefully, don't focus as thoroughly, and tend to be so focused on what is not yet done that they don't notice the mistakes they are making on what they are currently doing. Mistakes are still a form of feedback. The key is to understand what they are telling you. In this case, they are telling you that you are not managing time well.

Raw speed is not the answer.

THE PERFORMANCE CURVE

In any sport, one of the key skills is learning to focus on what matters and ignore what doesn't. A tired athlete tends to be slow and easily distracted; he has trouble focusing on his opponent, the team, or what is happening around him and so his reaction time is compromised. On the other hand, an athlete who is too energized shifts her attention faster than she can determine what is and what is not important. Eventually, the brain becomes exhausted and temporarily loses its ability to shift focus. This is tunnel vision.

Imagine the letter U written large and flipped over. The inverted U represents the performance curve, how our ability to focus and concentrate changes with how energized we're feeling. That state of being energized is technically known as our level of physiologic arousal, or simply arousal. The left side of the inverted U, representing sleep, is a state at which we do not focus very well. The far right side, or the red zone, is that state of tunnel vision that I just mentioned. On the right side, we're overenergized, hyper, or panicked. If you've ever felt that buzz from drinking too much coffee, that feeling that you can't sit still and can't focus, that's on the right side of the performance curve.

The optimal point is at the top of the curve. That is the point at which we are most able to ignore distractions and focus on what is actually important. It is the point at which we are most easily able to tell the difference between relevant and irrelevant inputs. This varies from task to task: the appropriate level of arousal is different for chess than for fencing, for operating machinery than for writing software. When we work our way up the curve, performance increases linearly. When we work our way down the right side of the curve, performance decreases linearly until it drops off a cliff.

Doing Well Under Stress

With the concept of the performance curve in mind, let's take a moment to understand what stress is and why some people seem to do so well under stress.

At a fundamental level, stress is what we call any demands on our time and energy that raise our level of arousal. Stress is something that activates our primitive responses to danger. How does this work? Consider the story of Og.

Once upon a time, around twenty-five thousand years ago, there lived a caveman named Og. Og probably spent his time hunting and trying not to be gathered. In the course of a busy day on the job, Og might have run into a saber-toothed tiger. Upon recognizing the danger he was in, Og would have immediately started producing adrenaline. Because his body would need every bit of energy it could find in order to survive, blood would be routed away from nonessential functions, such as digestion, and into his muscles. Heart rate and breathing would increase so that he could take in more oxygen and pump it out to the muscles. In short, Og would prepare to fight or run.

Fast-forward to today. Og's great-great-great, etc., grandson, Jefferson Herringbone-Smythe IV, is sitting in an office. Jefferson is not likely to run into any saber-toothed tigers in the course of his day. However, he might be told by the phone company that, "I'm sorry, sir, but our records show that you did call Outer Mongolia and speak for sixteen hours. The charge is $1,270.23 and is overdue." Or his boss might come in, screaming that he needed that report ten minutes ago. Or Jefferson may be cut off in traffic while rushing to a meeting. Or his computer might crash just as he was about to print that report.

In response to each of these situations, Jefferson's body would immediately start producing adrenaline. Heart rate and breathing would increase, blood would be routed away from nonessential functions, such as digestion, and into his muscles. In short, like Great-Granddaddy Og, Jefferson is preparing to fight or run.

It may seem a bit odd that Jefferson's response to a perceived threat is essentially identical to Og's. This response is the product of millions of years of evolution. The twenty-five thousand years between Og and Jefferson are a blink in evolutionary time. Give Og a shave, a haircut, and a good suit, and he could be anyone from janitor to CEO. Although life has changed a great deal since Og's day, how our bodies respond to threats has not.

This reaction, the fight-or-flight response, helps us survive sudden dangers. It puts the body into overdrive. Unfortunately, while Og gets to burn off his energy by running or bashing on the tiger, Jefferson does not get that option. Bashing in the head of one's boss is typically frowned upon, as is running screaming from the office. As a result, Jefferson is unable to meet the threat in the traditional fashion, and his body continues to act as though he is in danger.

What Jefferson is experiencing is, of course, stress. While stress is not inherently bad, how long it lasts and how we respond to it can be. Moving through the performance curve can be a positive. When we're on the left side, we want to move up to the top. However, when we're at the top, stress can cause us to overshoot and start moving down the right side. Furthermore, maintaining a state of high arousal is not healthy. When the body is constantly on red alert, blood pressure and heart rate remain elevated, digestion is hampered, and healing and the immune system are suppressed. This isn't generally a concern if the stress lasts for a few minutes or hours, but it becomes problematic when it lasts for days at a time, or longer. In the latter case, Jefferson could end up experiencing anything from indigestion and distractibility to more serious problems such as reduced attentional capacity, high blood pressure, and heart disease.

Jefferson's company, in turn, is the lucky recipient of reduced productivity and higher health care costs.

What Are the Signs of Stress in an Organization?

One of the big problems with stress in organizational settings is that we often adapt too easily. There is an apocryphal story that if you put a frog in boiling water, it'll jump out, but if you put it in cool water and slowly heat the water, the frog will sit there until it cooks. Actually, it turns out that the only way that a frog will sit there is if you equip it with little tiny cement galoshes. Frogs have enough sense to get out of the hot water.

Organizations, on the other hand, frequently have cultures that teach that stress is something to be ignored, that it's part of life, that you should just buck up and deal. There is even a great deal of truth to all of these beliefs. Stress is part of most jobs, and there will be periods of extreme stress in almost any project. The problem is not short-term stress, which people are very good at handling, provided there is adequate recovery time. The problem is long-term, persistent stress, which wears down the performance of an organization in much the same way as sand in the gears wears down the performance of a machine. Over time, the sand slowly degrades performance and increases friction until the machine either seizes up or explodes dramatically, much like the chicken-pie-making machine in *Chicken Run*.

The key to avoid this is to recognize the signs of persistent organizational stress early, before you get caught up in the organizational stress cycle:

- Motivation is driven by highlighting risks to the company.
- Employees are constantly reminded that they must work long hours in order to have any hope of corporate survival.
- Affiliation breaks down between teams. Each group retreats into its own metaphorical fortress.
- When the problems don't go away, affiliation between team members weakens, leading to further conflict.
- Constant fear narrows perspectives and keeps the business focused on short-term fixes instead of long-term problem solving and innovation.
- As communications break down, team members find it difficult or impossible to engage in constructive conversations. The increasing tension and suspicion cause people to view conversations as win/lose confrontations rather than opportunities for collaboration and cooperation. Force tends to generate force.
- Without effective communications, mistakes cease being useful as feedback and are instead compounded.
- Because of the perception that everything is an emergency, decision-making processes start to break down as anxiety increases. Discussion and debate decline, conflict is avoided, and decisions become increasingly reactive, short-sighted, and nonparticipatory.
- Interpersonal conflicts increase and, more and more frequently, remain unresolved. Team structure breaks down, with high-performance teams potentially collapsing back to Storming or Forming.
- As the situation deteriorates, authoritarian decision making becomes the norm. The tendency to resort to force is a strong one, and one that frequently emerges under conditions of high stress. Employees are increasingly seen as interchangeable components, not as individuals.
- As part of the overall tendency toward withdrawal, management becomes steadily more isolated from the rest of the company. Input from non-managers is assumed to have ulterior motives.
- Employees see management control as attacking their autonomy. They may respond by working fewer hours, spending more time on e-mail or surfing the Web, quietly discouraging potential new hires from accepting jobs at the company, etc. If people have not already started leaving the company, the exodus usually begins at this point.
- All parties become increasingly focused on surviving the conflict. The need for self-preservation becomes paramount, and the company's goals are forgotten.
- Disenchantment spreads throughout the company.

- Product quality decreases. Standards may also be lowered, to try to hide or deny the deterioration. Contempt for the customer is common.
- Some internal or external event triggers the final explosion. Small companies may simply go out of business; larger ones can lose entire teams or even divisions.

The key to effectively preventing the final explosion is intervening early and building a strong team foundation. The later the intervention, the harder it is to accomplish and the less likely it is to succeed. Once a company is in a power dive straight for the ground, it's generally too late to do anything.

We touched on some of the ways of managing stress as part of our discussion of motivation. Stress can also be managed by dealing with the physiological effects. Exercise, massage, and meditation are all techniques that can be used to help the body deal with stress and turn off the fight-or-flight response. They are all important, and it's worthwhile encouraging your employees to make use of them. If you truly believe that your people are your most valuable asset, then it's worth the investment to keep those assets in peak condition. Besides, all three of these stress management techniques also can improve creativity, innovation, and problem solving. The rest of this chapter, though, will focus on structuring time to minimize unnecessary stress.

YOU ONLY LIVE TWICE

If you happen to be Bond, James Bond, British agent 007, then you only live twice. The rest of us, of course, only live once. Despite the fact that we only live once, though, we talk all the time about work life and family life, as though these were two separate existences. They're not. The two are inextricably intertwined, which is why one of the major sources of stress for employees is work/family conflict.

If you continually put people in a position where they feel that they must regularly sacrifice family for work, then you reduce job satisfaction. Job satisfaction is key to maintaining organizational commitment. If you reduce job satisfaction, you reduce commitment, and therefore employees are less willing to put forth extra effort. If you try to bribe them or force them, you end up in the motivation trap. Instead, make it easy for them to have your way.

Recall that time is a way of rewarding people. When you encourage people to go home a little early if they're running ahead of schedule, or to leave the office to attend their kid's soccer game or school play, you are using time to build up a reservoir of good faith. This does, of course, require well-designed schedules, which we'll get to shortly.

When you demonstrate that you are willing to give employees time to meet their needs, it is much easier to ask them for time to meet the organization's needs. It's all about perception: if the organization is perceived as acting fairly, people are much more committed and willing to sacrifice on the part of it. More to the point, their families are much more willing to accept that sacrifice, removing a key element of work/family conflict.

Fundamentally, if you want loyalty, first demonstrate loyalty. If you want people to sacrifice for you, find opportunities to sacrifice for them first. If you want commitment, first demonstrate commitment. IBM's Tom Watson demonstrated these basic facts decades ago, and the lessons still hold true today. A big part of being a successful leader is demonstrating respect, appreciation, and fairness.

Conveying that sense of fairness lies mostly in how you communicate. The better a job you do at keeping people informed, the greater the level of perceived fairness. The trick, of course, is to balance access to information with overload. That means that not every communication is urgent; voice messages should be short, infrequent, and to the point; and there should be an easily accessible repository for important communications. Avoid the tendency to cry wolf. At one company, the general manager would regularly broadcast long, rambling voice mails and would always mark them urgent. They rarely were. Of course, employees became accustomed to ignoring the messages, or at least not listening very closely. When there was something important, no one noticed.

MAKING THE MOST OF MEETINGS

Let's look now at another way in which time evaporates in organizations: the infamous meeting. Meetings have a very bad reputation as major time-wasters. Their reputation stems from the fact that the 90 percent of meetings that are poorly run give a bad name to the remaining 10 percent. OK, I'm being a little tongue-in-cheek here, but the serious point is that a common problem is people spending hours in meetings and emerging bored, frustrated, and feeling like they've just wasted their day.

Meetings are popular in part because they create an illusion of progress. Although that illusion tends to evaporate in the cold, hard light of upcoming deadlines, when people are uncertain about how to proceed or feeling overwhelmed, meetings provide a degree of comfort and security. They make the person calling the meeting feel productive. This is especially common with managers or CEOs who feel a need to be constantly observing every step the team or company takes. The price for this comfort is time taken away from actual work, which leads to discomfort, and hence a desire to hold more meetings.

Meetings can also be a symptom of poor decision-making processes: holding a meeting helps to diffuse responsibility. A decision to hire, for example, cannot be blamed on any one person if the new hire doesn't work out. Unfortunately, in addition to diffusing blame, the mistake is not used as feedback to improve the hiring process, making the meeting doubly expensive.

Meetings are also common with early-stage teams, in which a sense of common ground, trust, and clear goals have not yet developed. Properly run meetings, in this case, can serve to help build the team and provide members with some necessary direction.

In businesses that have too many meetings, the greatest dangers are that too much work time will be lost and critical information will be lost in the noise—brought up in a meeting and quickly forgotten by people anxious to get back to work.

On the flip side, some companies refuse to hold any meetings. Oddly enough, this approach doesn't work either.

There are times when it can be very valuable to spend some focused time working on a problem with other people, exchanging ideas, or brainstorming. Not all information is easily conveyed over e-mail. In businesses that have no meetings, the greatest danger is that time will be wasted trying to figure out what to do and critical information will never be communicated.

In fact, the two extreme positions of too many meetings or too few meetings produce remarkably similar results, none of them good. Autonomy is the result of having enough structure, not too little and not too much.

The goal, in other words, is to have exactly as many meetings as are necessary, control their length, and make them work.

Do You Need to Hold This Meeting?

Hold only meetings that are actually important. Ask yourself what purpose the meeting is serving and if there is a more efficient way to accomplish the same thing. For example, status meetings make managers feel good but achieve little else. Instead, encourage the relevant people to send out brief e-mail announcements whenever they complete a task. Everyone will have the information in their inbox instead of having to remember it.

Establish Your Goals for the Meeting

Have an agenda and make sure the agenda makes sense. Know ahead of time what you want to accomplish in the meeting, and make sure the important items are dealt with first. Don't let the meeting wander off in search of a topic. If you find that there are agenda items that never get dealt with and never go away, either schedule time to deal with them or drop them. You can set a time limit on any such "carry on" items so that you know when they've become carrion and you can drop them before they start to smell.

Start on Time

Most people don't do anything right before a meeting because they know that they'll be interrupted. If the meeting starts late, employees will lose time waiting. Habitually starting meetings late gives the message that you don't care about your employees' time, thus decreasing motivation and affiliation. At one company, the weekly 4 P.M. company meeting always started late except when the CEO wandered out at 4:15 to announce that it wasn't being held. This did not endear him to anyone.

All's Well That Ends

Limit the meeting duration in advance. This helps keep you honest and keeps people focused. It also lets people plan their day better, allowing for more productive use of time. When an hour meeting takes two hours, people will spend that second hour figuring out how they're going to reorganize their day. It's better to make a habit of budgeting more time than you think you'll need and ending early. That always gives people a very real sense of accomplishment.

What Goes in Must Come Out

If your meeting is going to last longer than an hour or so, make sure you take breaks. Give people a chance to think, stretch, get coffee and snacks, and so on. Don't forget to put in bathroom breaks, especially if people are drinking a lot of coffee! Knowing there's a break coming up is all most people need to be patient. Otherwise, people will either be wandering in and out of the meeting, or they'll be somewhat distracted. People are not productive when they're thinking about their bladders. Brainstorming meetings require regular breaks to keep people's minds fresh and creative.

Moderate the Discussion

Whether you're running a design meeting or brainstorming session, don't allow one or two very vocal people to dominate the discussion. Quiet people can have good ideas too. Especially in early-stage teams, it's common to have the vocal and the reticent. If you allow that to become the pattern, then you'll lose valuable input from the start. If the discussion starts to drag or you have trouble getting people to contribute, come up with process goals: for example, everyone come up with three ways to analyze this data or three interpretations of what this problem might mean.

Did You Accomplish Your Goals?

After the meeting, review it and see if you accomplished the goals you defined at the beginning. If not, that's feedback. Take the time to understand why you didn't accomplish the goals. Were they inappropriate or incorrect goals, was the process poor, was the meeting unnecessary, or did you allow the meeting to wander off in search of a topic? Adjust accordingly.

Running a meeting is, at root, a simple version of a more complex problem: scheduling.

SCHEDULING SUCCESS

We talk a lot about schedules in business: Are we on schedule? Are we ahead of schedule? I've found that everyone expects to be behind schedule, but hardly anyone expects to be ahead of schedule. This is extremely unfortunate, because being consistently behind schedule tells you that there's a problem with the scheduling process!

Ultimately, a schedule is not a device to make sure that each person is working every minute, nor is it a device to enable you to know what everyone is doing every minute of the day. Rather, a schedule is a tool for managing time. It is a device for making sure that we don't try to do everything all at once and a way of making sure that everything we need is in the right place at the right time.

I made that statement in a seminar I was teaching, and one project manager became extremely irate. He interrupted to go on a long rant about how you could apply advanced statistical techniques to calculate the exact time each piece of the project would take, assemble a schedule accordingly, and guarantee that the deadline would be hit on the nose. When he was finished, I asked him what would happen to his schedule if someone got the flu. He stared at me like he'd never heard of the flu before. I found out later that his projects were legendary for missing their deadlines.

Apparently the flu is unimpressed by advanced statistical techniques.

What Are the Features of a Good Schedule?

A key component of goal-setting is time. A schedule is an implementation of your goals. It is the time component broken down, analyzed, and organized. It is the structuring of your proximal and distal goals. In short, a schedule is a tool for accomplishing goals. Thus, a good schedule has a lot in common with a good goal. As with goals, the trick is to hit the appropriate level of challenge. Increasing the difficulty of a goal increases motivation, right up until people start perceiving the goal as impossible, at which point motivation decreases. Similarly, an aggressive schedule gets people excited, but too aggressive gets people discouraged. The goal is a schedule that is sufficiently challenging that people are motivated to work hard, yet easy enough that people will generally be able to beat the schedule. Being ahead of schedule gets people far more excited and builds far more momentum than being behind. Excited people have this tendency to succeed far more often than do discouraged ones.

The higher the performance of your team, the more the concept of the eight-hour day or forty-hour week is an illusion. When people are excited by the work and committed to the vision, they put in the time and effort necessary. Your schedule needs to be specific enough to know that you're on track and broad enough to give people as much autonomy as possible. Some teams and some team members may favor higher intensity for shorter times, others lower intensity for longer periods of time. Some teams will take more breaks than others. It depends very much on the level of team development, the personalities of the people, and the nature of the project. Your schedule needs to take this into account and also be prepared to deal with the changing, and hopefully improving, dynamic of your team. As a general rule, teams that work at higher levels of intensity will need more breaks, whether or not they believe that. Like the Tour de France, if you give your all on the first stage or in the first few stages, you won't make it to the finish.

A good schedule also has to balance two other competing demands: you need to define clear milestones and know how you'll measure success or failure of each milestone. Preferably, you can define your criteria well in advance, although sometimes you can only define criteria for the first milestone. In that case, part of the milestone is defining your criteria for the next milestone! At the same time, you also need to allow enough flexibility in the schedule to deal with the unexpected. Some tasks may turn out to be much easier or, more commonly, much harder than expected. A simple one-man project may become a complex multi-person project.

Fundamentally, beating your schedule is motivating. Being behind schedule is demotivating. When a team is behind schedule, there is an almost palpable sense of tension and panic in the area. You're pushing your team into the red zone.

A team in the red zone is less able to handle unexpected problems, less innovative, less able to produce high-quality work. A team that's beating the schedule, on the other hand, comes to work excited to tackle the challenges of the day. They are usually bubbling over with ideas and eager to look for ways to improve the process. Changes, new information, or adjustments to the schedule are viewed with enthusiasm, not a sense of dread.

A very powerful, extremely effective way to build a schedule is to use a structured system that can, with only a few contortions, be captured in the acronym FRAMES.

Flu Factor

The first part of the frame is the flu factor, or respecting Murphy's Law. Part of designing an effective schedule is being able to cope with unexpected shocks. If every problem or delay is a crisis, you've got a problem. When designing a schedule, you always have to ask yourself, what will happen if a key member of the team gets the flu? Do you really want that person coming into the office and working anyway? Then your whole team can have the flu! Isn't sharing wonderful?

By extension, it's important to look at possible disruptors and make sure that they won't derail your entire project. If you live in the northeast United States, you can bet that at least one major winter storm will shut down roads and make travel difficult or impossible. Sometimes roads are shut down by torrential rains. Florida has hurricanes. I could go on, but the key point is that these are all predictable, routine issues. They happen every year. Assuming that they won't is just plain silly. Snowstorms happen, so build some slush into the schedule right from the start.

If you know that your office is going to move in the middle of the project, build that in. Always allow more time for the move than you think you'll need! It takes a little while for office routines to settle down after a big move.

At two of the companies I worked for many years ago, we had big office moves during major projects. In both cases, the engineering team was told that the movers would show up by 9 A.M. and that the computers would be set up and ready for us to work at the new location by noon. In both cases, the movers were late, there were problems getting things set up at the new office, and we ended up sitting around for hours getting more and more frustrated. No work was done that day, and people were still stressed and grumpy the next day. It would have made more sense to just acknowledge the day would be lost and give everyone a day off. Demonstrating that you care about people on your team is a powerful way of building affiliation and increasing motivation.

Realistic

Make sure that your schedule is realistic. An overly optimistic schedule produces a pessimistic team, while a mildly pessimistic schedule produces an optimistic and highly motivated team. You want the latter.

This is the time to avoid best-case scenarios and focus on the things that can go wrong. It's not disloyal to ask questions or raise concerns.

For a schedule to be realistic, the team has to be moving at a pace that it can maintain for the long term. If you start out working twelve-hour days, you won't make it to the finish line. People cannot maintain that pace and be productive for more than a few days at a time, if that.

When your schedule is too optimistic, you end up working those longer hours and being more prone to error. The team also wastes energy and time reacting to artificial emergencies. Missing an arbitrary deadline is not an emergency! It is merely feedback. If it keeps happening, your schedule is not realistic. You need to take the time to figure out why not: Do you lack resources? Is your team not yet capable of working together well? Is your team discouraged by the task? Are you moving too quickly?

If you burn out your team early, you have no energy for real emergencies. They will happen. No matter how well you plan, no matter what you do, something will take longer than it seems like it should. A vendor will provide defective material, or you'll discover a bug in a critical piece of software. A realistic schedule recognizes that excessive optimism is a recipe for disaster.

At the start of a project, it's often difficult or impossible to accurately assess how long each step will take. Therefore, it's important to start slowly and increase speed as you go. With each step, the team becomes more confident and better at estimating how long the next steps will take.

Avoid Scope Creep

The death of many a project is scope creep. It's always tempting to add just one more thing, do just a little more, and so on.

Allowing unplanned-for items to be added to the schedule willy-nilly is a recipe for trouble. For example, you may find yourself with poorly designed features that detract from the product. People will be more upset by something that doesn't work than by something that isn't there. The former is a constant irritant, while the latter is an eagerly anticipated hope for the future.

Part of schedule design is defining milestones and identifying how you'll know if you're on or off course. When you allow scope creep, you are adding things to the schedule without the safety net of having thought through and evaluated the steps.

Measure and Celebrate Progress

A key element of scheduling is defining, in advance, how you'll measure progress. When a team member thinks she's done a great deal, there are few things more frustrating, and demotivating than being told that she is being evaluated according to a measure she didn't realize was important.

Defining your measurement methods is not always simple. Like goals, you generally want to look at outputs rather than inputs. For example, are you measuring in terms of results achieved or hours put in? Many businesses claim the former but actually use the latter.

A clear ruler means that team members can constantly gauge their own progress; they'll know whether they need to work more to meet a deadline. By giving people the tools to allocate their time, you are building their autonomy and sense of competence. You are exhibiting strong leadership behaviors and increasing the motivation and dedication of your team.

Another advantage of having a clearly defined ruler is that you know how the team is doing without being obtrusive in obtaining that information. Developing a good schedule with clearly defined standards for measuring progress and clearly defined milestones is a big part of creating the structure that permits autonomy.

If someone is running ahead of schedule, don't "reward" that person by slapping on more work. Let him relax a bit. Remember, different people work at different speeds and differing levels of intensity. Someone who works rapidly and intensely will still be tired when he's done.

Take the time to periodically celebrate your progress. Remember, it's always more motivating and encouraging to see how far up the mountain you've climbed than how far there is still to go. Being able to agree upon progress is critical to believing the progress you've made.

If you can't define all your milestones or measurements up front, that's OK! It just means that identifying and defining how you'll measure future milestones needs to be part of your milestones. As you move forward and gain more information, you'll be able to adjust your measurement criteria as the more distant milestones move into focus.

Elastic

Different people will work at different rates. Within a milestone, different people may have different deadlines: Ivan Tadeov may need to finish his section before Franz MacLisp can do his.

On one software project, the people doing database back end needed to finish their pieces before the people doing the front end could finish their work. The database engineers would finish and take a break while the front-end developers went to work. The front-end developers would constantly scream that the database guys were slacking off. From the point of view of the front-end folks, they were the only ones working hard!

Your schedule needs to be structured to allow for the inherently uneven paces that may develop.

Specific

Like a goal, a schedule needs to be specific. You need to know what you're trying to accomplish, by when, and what your milestones are. The dependencies between, and even within, your milestones must be clearly identified. Dependencies within teams and between teams must be clearly identified as well.

Now it may seem odd that I specified that "by when" is a component of the schedule. After all, I've tended to be fairly dismissive of specific time measures to this point.

No project is open-ended. No matter what you are doing, there's probably someone somewhere who expects it by a certain date. You may be coating medical devices for a customer, coordinating the shipment of a software suite among different branches of the company, or building an office complex. There's always a deadline.

Part of scheduling is working backward from the deadline to the present and identifying what steps you need to take and how you'll know you've accomplished them. You need to know if everything you want to do will fit in the time available. If it won't, you need to scale back or push back the "due date." On the other hand, if your schedule leaves too much time at the end, you should make sure you're being pessimistic enough. Are you making unreasonable assumptions? If so, adjust and reevaluate. If you still have extra time, you can look at shortening the schedule, adding additional features, or taking a vacation at the end.

Early milestones should be smaller, getting bigger as you progress. The idea is to build successes from the start and thereby build momentum for your team.

Remember, the goal of a schedule is not to move fast, it's to make sure that everything is in the right place at the right time.

The Illusion of Time

Time is still an illusion, but it's an illusion that can work for you or against you. The more you fight time, the harder you make the job for everyone. Instead, make time work for you. It takes some effort, but the results are well worth the, ahem, time invested.

DEVELOPING YOUR ORGANIZATION

When it comes to building a successful organization, there are no magic bullets: you cannot lead through magic spells. Like success in sports or martial arts, success takes an understanding of what works and what does not, and a great deal of consistent, steady effort. This book is and can be only a beginning step in your ongoing mastery of your own organization. If you have questions or would like more information on any of the topics I've covered, feel free to visit my blog, www.TheBusinessSensei.com, or my website, www.7stepsahead.com.

In the end, your organization will be a reflection of you and your approach to leadership. You will shape the culture of your company, and that culture will, in turn, shape you. The more intentional you are about shaping that culture, the more successful you will be. Experiment. Take some risks. Make mistakes. Act, not react. Ask questions. Just as in the practice of jujitsu, there's always something more to learn.

If you take nothing else from this book, learn to see your organization as a collection of moving, interacting parts. If you keep the gears well oiled and remember to make it easy for your employees to have your way, you're well on the way to creating a world-class organization.

I'll leave you with two questions:

1. What three things can you do (or start doing) right now to make your organization more successful and your employees more motivated?
2. What's stopping you?

Review Quiz

1. **The goal of a schedule is to**
   a. Make sure everyone is working
   b. Make sure you can account for every instant of time
   c. Know who the slackers are
   d. Make sure everything is in the right place at the right time
   e. a & c
2. **Stress**
   a. Can activate the fight-or-flight response
   b. Is a healthy way to generate productivity
   c. Encourages innovation
   d. Is just part of life, so deal with it
   e. b & c
3. **Techniques for effectively dealing with the physiological effects of stress include**
   a. Exercise
   b. Meditation
   c. Massage

   d. a & b

   e. a, b, & c

4. **Part of running a good meeting includes**
   a. Having an agenda
   b. Sticking to the time allotted
   c. Having goals
   d. Moderating the discussion
   e. All of the above

5. **A good schedule**
   a. Has a flu factor built in
   b. Is rigid and unchanging
   c. Can have every milestone defined at the start
   d. Does not involve people
   e. All of the above

6. **A realistic schedule is one that**
   a. Can be maintained over the long term
   b. Has every time interval calculated using advanced statistical techniques
   c. Has people constantly falling behind
   d. Does not accept changing circumstances
   e. Is short

BIBLIOGRAPHY

Balzac, Stephen. "Reality from Fantasy: Using Predictive Scenarios to Explore Ethical Dilemmas." In *Ethics and Game Design: Teaching Values Through Play*, edited by David Gibson and Karen Schrier. New York: IGI, 2010.

Benson, Herbert. *The Relaxation Response*. New York: HarperCollins, 1975.

Benson, Herbert, and William Proctor. *Beyond the Relaxation Response*. New York: Berkley, 1984.

Benson, Herbert, and William Proctor. *The Breakout Principle*. New York: Scribner, 2003.

Cox, Richard. *Sport Psychology: Concepts and Applications*. 5th ed. New York: McGraw-Hill, 2002.

Csikszentmihalyi, Mihaly. *Flow: The Psychology of Optimal Experience*. New York: Harper Collins, 1990.

Fisher, Roger, William L. Ury, and Bruce Patton. *Getting to Yes*. 2nd ed. New York: Penguin Books, 1991.

Gollwitzer, Peter M., and Veronika Brandstätter. "Implementation Intentions and Effective Goal Pursuit." *Journal of Personality and Social Psychology* 73(1997): 186–199.

Gollwitzer, Peter M. "Implementation Intentions: Strong Effects of Simple Plans." *American Psychologist* 54(1999): 493–503.

Hater, John J., and Bernard M. Bass. "Superiors' Evaluations and Subordinates' Perceptions of Transformational and Transactional Leadership." *Journal of Applied Psychology* 73(1988): 695–702.

Kark, Ronit, Boas Shamir, and Gilad Chen. "The Two Faces of Transformational Leadership: Empowerment and Dependency." *Journal of Applied Psychology* 88(2003): 246–255.

Kirkpatrick, Shelley A., and Edwin A. Locke. "Direct and Indirect Effects of Three Core Charismatic Leadership Components on Performance and Attitudes." *Journal of Applied Psychology* 81(1996): 36–51.

Koestner, Richard, Natasha Lekes, Theodore A. Powers, and Emanuel Chicoine. "Attaining Personal Goals: Self-Concordance Plus Implementation Intentions Equals Success." *Journal of Personality and Social Psychology* 83(2002): 231–244.

Latham, Gary P., and Edwin A. Locke. "New Developments in and Directions for Goal-Setting Research." *European Psychologist* 12(4)(2007): 290–300.

Locke, Edwin A., and Gary P. Latham. "Building a Practically Useful Theory of Goal Setting and Task Motivation: A 35-Year Odyssey." *American Psychologist* 57(9)(2002): 705–717.

Mandell, Barbara, and Shilpa Pherwani. "Relationship Between Emotional Intelligence and Transformational Leadership Style: A Gender Comparison." *Journal of Business and Psychology* 17(2003): 387–404.

Marsh, Richard L., Jason L. Hicks, and Martin L. Bink. "Activation of Completed, Uncompleted, and Partially Completed Intentions." *Journal of Experimental Psychology: Learning, Memory, and Cognition* 24(1998): 350–361.

Miller, William R., and Stephen Rollnick. *Motivational Interviewing.* 2nd ed. New York: Guilford Press, 2002.

Pentland, Alex. *Honest Signals: How They Shape Our World.* Cambridge MA: MIT Press, 2008.

Peterson, Randall S., D. Brent Smith, Paul V. Martorana, and Pamela D. Owens. "The Impact of Chief Executive Officer Personality on Top Management Team Dynamics: One Mechanism by Which Leadership Affects Organizational Performance." *Journal of Applied Psychology* 88(2003): 795–808.

Schein, Edgar H. "Organizational Culture." *American Psychologist* 45(2) (1990): 109–119.

Schein, Edgar H. "Three Cultures of Management: The Key to Organizational Learning." *Sloan Management Review* 38(1)(1996): 9–20.

Schein, Edgar H. *The Corporate Culture Survival Guide.* San Francisco: Jossey-Bass, 1999.

Schein, Edgar H. "Five Traps for Consulting Psychologists or, How I Learned to Take Culture Seriously." *Consulting Psychology Journal: Practice and Research* 55(2)(2003): 75–83.

Schein, Edgar H. *Helping: How to Offer, Give, and Receive Help*. San Francisco: Berrett-Koehler, 2009.

Seijts, Gerard, and Gary P. Latham. "The Effects of Goal Setting and Group Size on Performance in a Social Dilemma." *Canadian Journal of Behavioural Science* 32(2)(2000): 104–116.

Sheldon, Kennon M., and Andrew J. Elliot. "Goal Striving, Need Satisfaction, and Longitudinal Well-Being: The Self-Concordance Model." *Journal of Personality and Social Psychology* 76(1999): 482–497.

Turner, Nick, Julian Barling, Olga Epitropaki, Vicky Butcher, and Caroline Milner. "Transformational Leadership and Moral Reasoning." *Journal of Applied Psychology* 87(2002): 304–311.

Ury, William. *Getting Past No*. New York: Bantam, 1991.

Useem, Michael. *The Leadership Moment*. New York: Three Rivers Press, 1998.

Wheelan, Susan A. *Group Processes: A Developmental Perspective*. 2nd ed. Boston: Allyn & Bacon, 2005.

Yukl, Gary. *Leadership in Organizations*. 5th ed. Upper Saddle River, NJ: Prentice-Hall, 2002.

Zimbardo, Philip, and John Boyd. *The Time Paradox*. New York: Free Press, 2008.

INDEX

INSTRUCTIONS FOR ACCESSING ONLINE FINAL EXAM AND CHAPTER QUIZ ANSWERS

I f you have completed your study of *The McGraw-Hill 36-Hour Course: Organizational Development*, you should be prepared to take the online final examination. It is a comprehensive test, consisting of 65 multiple-choice questions. You may treat this test as an "open book" exam by consulting this book and any other resources. Answers to both the online exam and the chapter-ending quizzes can be found on The McGraw-Hill 36-Hour Course Information Center landing site for each book (please see the instructions below for accessing the site).

Instructions for Accessing Online Final Exam
1. Go to www.36hourbooks.com.
2. Once you arrive on the home page, scroll down until you find The McGraw-Hill 36-Hour Course: Organizational Development and

click the link "Test your skills here." At this point you will be redirected to The McGraw-Hill 36-Hour Course Information Center landing site for the book.

3. Click the "Click Here to Begin" button in the center of the landing site. You will be brought to a page containing detailed instructions for taking the final exam and obtaining your Certificate of Achievement.

4. Click on "Self-Assessment Quiz" in the left-hand navigation bar to begin the exam.

Instructions for Accessing Answers to Chapter-Ending Quizzes

1. Follow Steps 1 and 2 above.
2. Click "Chapter-Ending Quiz Answers" in the left-hand navigation bar.

ABOUT THE AUTHOR

Stephen R. Balzac, "The Business Sensei," is a consultant and professional speaker. He is the president of 7 Steps Ahead, LLC (www.7stepsahead.com), a consulting firm specializing in helping businesses to increase their revenue and build their client base through improving individual, team, and organizational performance.

Steve has more than twenty years of experience in the high-tech industry and is the former director of operations for Silicon Genetics, in Redwood City, California, where he was responsible for shipping its flagship product. Steve led the development of numerous serious role-playing simulations, including a Pandemic Flu simulation for the U.S. National Capitol Region. He is a popular speaker on topics ranging from leadership, motivation, team building, innovation, and sports performance to computer game design. His articles have appeared in a number of journals, including *Journal of Interactive Drama*, *IBM Systems Journal*, *Mass High Tech*, *Enterprise Management Quarterly*, *The CEO Refresher*, *Journal of Corporate Recruiting Leadership*, *Analog SF/F*, and *Worcester Business Journal*. Steve is a contributing author to *Ethics and Game Design: Teaching Values Through Play*. He is a frequent radio guest and is often quoted in a variety of publications.

Steve serves on the board of the New England Society of Applied Psychology (NESAP) and is the president of the Society of Professional Consultants (SPC). No stranger to the challenges of achieving peak performance under competitive and stressful conditions, he holds a fourth degree black belt in jujitsu and is a former nationally ranked competitive fencer.

Building effective development organizations; improving team morale, focus, and enthusiasm; developing effective communications among team members; reducing employee turnover; helping businesses identify and attain strategic targets; and applying sports psychology techniques to business have been some of his most successful projects.

Steve has a bachelor's and a master's degree in computer science and engineering from MIT, and a master's degree in industrial/organizational psychology from Capella University. He is an adjunct professor of industrial/organizational psychology at the Wentworth Institute of Technology in Boston, Massachusetts.

Steve lives in Stow, Massachusetts, with his wife, two children, and two very persistent cats.